T0165383

I Found GOD In HOLLYWOOD

Cliff Brodsky

"A searingly honest and funny account of an artist's journey. Through a mostly affectionate look back at his adventures, the author illuminates the formation of a young man's character and the inspirations for his love of music."

Christopher Vogler
Story Consultant and Author of *The Writer's Journey*

"A winsome chronicle of interesting life experiences and colorful characters; as if the "everyman" in Brodsky just can't help wandering through the looking glass from time to time. The mundane, the artistic and the bizarre combine in these encounters...pleasingly both twisted and charming."

Jim Martone
President, Suitable Group, LLC

"Brodsky has created an off beat, fun filled, walk through of all the aspects of his rock' n roll life. This guy tells it like it is, from his love affair with playing piano, to picking up the pieces of a rock band on tour. A must read for those with a passion for the arts."

Bill Pfordresher
Producer/Songwriter

"They say every sinner has a future and every saint has a past. Cliff's journey in 'I Found God in Hollywood' is a sublime example that getting into trouble can sometimes be the best path towards finding that sweet place of bliss we all are searching for. If you can find God in Hollywood, you can find It pretty much anywhere else!"

Mastin Kipp
CEO of the Love Yourself Company and TheDailyLove.com

TABLE of CONTENTS

dedicated to **Neda**

my number one fan and only fan, but
as long as I have ONE fan, I'm good

Acknowledgments

I'd like to thank all the people who were mean to me, who didn't believe in me, who made my life a living hell; without them, I certainly wouldn't have made it this far.

Credits

Edited by David Tabatsky
Illustrations by James Gulliver Hancock
Back Cover Photo by Anthony Mongiello

Introduction

This book is a collection of some of my personal favorite stories that are 98% true. I chose the most charged, energized, and quite frankly, in my opinion some of the more strange things that have happened to me. For some weird reason, I feel that the world needs to know who I am, where I come from and the thoughts that are in my head.

I have chosen a sort of sophomoric, A.D.D. style of writing on *purpose* mainly because it is really easy for me to write like that and its the fastest way I can think of to get this book finished. Plus its a style that I think a good sized chunk of people will relate to. It is organized into four parts, that I consider to be pivotal in my life. Though it may seem that this book is a vanity project, and in many ways it is, it's really supposed to be funny. Many of the subjects are not 'technically' funny, but I have a strange sense of humor and to ME they're funny. Hopefully, more than one person will laugh out loud to *at least* one of my jokes. If not, then, I guess the jokes on me.

Anyway, the parts are organized in four sections, with part one being about growing up in Hanover N.H. in the 70's and early 80's. I had to whittle down just my best stories, because I can think of at least 20 more in each section, so, believe it or not, SOME editing has transpired. Even though to many readers it will seem like this entire book was written off the cuff, in one draft, with no proof reading, or any actual work other than just ranting and raving. However, there are *some* rants and raves, but they have been carefully crafted to be related to the actual stories and not just adding more CO_2 to the already overburden ionosphere.

Part two is about a few of my best experiences in Boston going to college at Berklee. Not the one up north in California, but the one named after Lawrence Berk who started a pretty cool music school way back in the 50's; maybe you've heard of it? Quincy Jones went there, so did Steely Dan and even John Mayer.

Part three is about my adventures in Hollywood. Driving to Hollywood, finding work, doing gigs, playing, teaching, touring, going insane; its all in there. And part four is about my life in Los Angeles *after* I got sober. You know, that means to stop the drugs and alcohol and all that FUN behavior. This is not a 12-Step approved book and I don't represent AA or any other fellowship in this book, though, I would like to say that I would be dead, in jail, or clinically insane if it weren't for AA and all the other programs that I have participated in.

Remember now, this is a FUNNY book, and has been carefully designed to make you laugh, out loud, more than once. Every story has a comedic thread throughout, and though it may seem like a 14-year-old man-boy wrote this in his AA journal in his first 6 weeks of sobriety, that simply is NOT the case. This book has been slaved over for 5 years and has been edited three times and a lot of money, time, and pain has been invested in this...dare I say...masterpiece? I want people to say that this book belongs on the same shelf as Mark Twain, Kurt Vonnegut Jr. and Richard Bach. Or at least say that it's in the same genre. Or maybe people will say its better, why should I shoot low? My guess is that most people won't get it, and only a few *enlightened individuals* (kind of like in the Emperors New Clothes story), will have the vision, insight, and intelligence to understand the comedic genius. Or maybe some people will like it and others won't, kind of like how most creative things are.

The main goal of this book is to spread a little joy, maybe make some people laugh and have a good time. If, for some reason, you get a little more understanding of your own life, or see something that raises your awareness some, then that's just extra credit.

Part Four is *after* I get sober in Hollywood and all the

fun and games and adventure is included, for free. You might even be amazed at what you might find in this book. Don't forget that sometimes we can find deep meaning and spirituality in some of the most random and superficial places; like Hollywood California.

PART ONE

Hanover N.H.

The Piano

When I was in 6th Grade I saw Alan Breed play the piano during recess. He was one grade ahead of me and his mother was the local piano teacher. He was also my next-door neighbor. I was jealous of him because he could play "Wipeout" on the

piano and all the cute girls were very impressed and gave him a lot of attention. I wasn't good at hardly anything, except being a nerd. Something really deep inside of me needed to be good at something; I needed to be special. So I chose the piano. I knew I was going to get good at that. I don't know how, but I just knew. Probably because I wanted to show Alan Breed that I was better than him and mainly because I wanted the attention of those cute girls. I think that's the real reason why I became a musician: so I could get girls.

The first song I have any memory of seeing or knowing about was "Wipeout." When Alan Breed played that, all the kids thought he was a genius. More important, the pretty girls thought he was cool.

It was pretty impressive. He could play it with two hands. But that's *all* he could play. He was a one-trick pony. But it didn't matter to anyone because back in those days that's all you needed to know to break the ice with all the cute chicks.

I just needed my own way to break the ice. I still need that (when there isn't a piano around). If there is, I'm basically all set. That is, unless there's another piano player who's better than me, then I'm really sunk. I hate to admit it, but if a really good piano player is around me, I get really insecure and feel like I'm not special anymore. It's terrible. I'm basically like Superman unless there's Kryptonite around (like another piano player who's better than me). When that happens, I'm unable to breath, speak, or defend myself. Certainly NOT able to walk up to a pretty chick and break the ice. Because, as we all know, taking the risk of being told to buzz off is one of the most horrifying experiences anyone could ever go through.

I came home from school that day and asked my mother if I could take piano lessons from Mrs. Breed. She said, why, of course you can. My mom wasn't excited or happy for me; she was just like, okay, why not? My request came out of the blue and she was just very nonchalant about it. Little did she know at that time how my life would end up as a direct result of my love for the piano.

When I started with Mrs. Breed, there were only two weeks left in her teaching cycle with a big recital coming at the end. She took me on anyway. Mrs. Breed was a great little piano teacher, even though (I found out later) she had a lot of trouble with her husband with alcoholism and of course her son ended up getting into drugs, etc. Alan didn't take lessons from his mother; he was a total rebel and was always in trouble with the authorities. He was always getting kicked out of prep schools and stuff.

Even though there were only two weeks left, I had to play some little dinky songs in front of all the other kids and parents. I remember it was the John Thompson Piano Method, Book One, and I must have only been on page five or six. I was totally scared, and I could barely play, but somehow I showed up. Of course my mother was there and she turned out to be very proud of me. There were probably 15 students all together with an assortment of moms and dads.

Some of the kids were really good and I was jealous that they could play so well. One of them was Chinese and I could tell that she practiced ALL THE TIME because there's no other way she could have been as good as she was. She could play "Flight Of The Bumblebee" and it was very impressive.

Most of the kids were older than me and MUCH better players. Some of them were my age, though. I had a crush on Pam Holbrook and Nancy Solow who were both students there at the time. Maybe I stayed on because I wanted to impress those two.

I always had little crushes on girls as far back as I can remember. I even had a crush on my kindergarten teacher, Miss Blackstone. I used to tell her that I would write her love letters as soon as I knew how to read and write. I even ended up writing to her all the way through second grade until my infatuation wore off.

I got really good really fast at the piano. My parents NEVER told me to practice. I practiced because from the get go I just loved playing. I worked really hard and there is NO substitute for working really hard at something in this life. That's how it was with me.

It didn't take long before I excelled. I knew that I had something special right away. I would run home from Mrs. Breed's house after my lesson because I couldn't wait to try all the new stuff I was learning. I also could play by ear and figure things out from memory by listening to the radio. I used to spend long hours at night in bed with a little radio listening to all those great old songs from the early '70's: Donny Osmond, The Jackson 5, The Partridge Family... whatever was on the radio would do, I didn't care. I pretty much liked all those old songs. I lived in a private little world and I connected with it like nothing I had ever experienced before.

In less than a year's time I knew how to read music well enough that I could understand how to play simple pop tunes. I had a great ear and could figure things out really fast, too. Between having a great ear and being able to read some, I had a lot of freedom and power. I'd buy big fat piano songbooks of the '70's with 100 songs in them and learn about 20 of my favorite ones right away. Songs like, "Go Away, Little Girl," "Theme from M.A.S.H.," "Tubular Bells," "Aquarius," "I Write The Songs," "Bennie And The Jets," "Piano Man" — all those cool old songs.

If I had heard a song before and liked it, I was able to play it by memory and be able to read enough of the chords and melodies and figure out the rest by teaching myself how it went. I learned hundreds of songs that way. I still do this today. I probably know 5,000 songs from memory.

The piano I learned on was really crappy. I mean REALLY crappy. It was out of tune, had a couple chipped keys, and barely worked. In fact, it was a full half step flat and not even concert pitch. Basically, any chance I would've had of being able to learn perfect pitch was shattered by that out-of-tune, flat piano. Maybe I resent my parents more for that simple fact than anything else they may have done that bothered me. Chain me to a fence and beat me, electrocute me and torture me, but don't make me practice on a piano that is out of concert pitch! Didn't they know how sensitive my little ears were?

I mentioned this dire fact to my parents as soon as I found out how out of tune that raggedy piano was and all they would say was stuff like, "Life isn't fair," or "You're lucky to be alive," or "Think of all the starving people in China."

The piano tuner would come over to our house every now and then and he'd tell me stuff about how bad the piano was and that it was destroying my ear. He somehow would make the piano get in tune with itself, so that if you didn't know any better it sounded sort of okay. I managed to have a pretty good ear, even if it was a half step flat.

Not only did my parents tell me ridiculous stuff about starving people in China, my mom even used to tell me that the crusts on toast had the most nutrition and that's why I had to eat them. The truth is, crusts on burnt toast have ZERO nutritional value and are basically empty calories and a form of food torture to a little kid.

I would never abuse a child like that. We even had a rule at the dinner table that you had to eat everything on your plate, even if it made you sick or if you could barely tolerate it.

I could tell that I had talent. Anyone with talent knows they have it because it's plain obvious. Would I show off? You bet your ass I would! Any chance I could play a piano in front of any audience of any kind I was there. If I was at a friend's house, I would always ask if they had a piano and if they did I'd manage to find my way over there and just start playing. I'd always make a good impression with everyone, especially the moms.

For some reason, I always used to be friends with my friends' moms. I even had a few crushes on a couple of them. I think they thought it was cute. My friend, Kristy Holland, had a super hot mom. I would go over there and complement her and tell her how pretty she was. She thought I was SO cute for that and loved all my little compliments and flirting. She would say that I was going to be very handsome when I grew up. I liked hearing that, and she just fueled me to go further into the flirting thing.

I used to practice a lot because I loved the piano so much. I still do. It's probably saved my life 100 times. I used to practice so much that I'd just keep going and going until I'd lose total track of time. It would be time for dinner and my step-dad would yell from upstairs, "Dinnertime, get up here!" and I'd keep going and going until I nearly got into actual trouble for interfering with dinnertime.

My first musical influence was Chico Marx, from the Marx Brothers. I used to watch a lot of television and always liked funny movies, like the Marx Brothers and Jerry Lewis.

Chico Marx fascinated me. I'd heard he was an

13

excellent pianist in real life, but he could also do so many other very impressive things. He could play the piano with his feet and had these funny hand gestures like Art Carney from *The Honeymooners*, which used to crack me up.

Of course I was totally obsessed with Elvis Presley—who wasn't? The funny thing was, pretty much everyone in my family didn't care about Elvis like I did, except for my sister, Breena. When Elvis was on TV, one of us would scream for the other to run downstairs to the basement so we could watch our hero on the black and white TV. My sister and I would spend hours together watching tons of old, cheesy movies with Elvis, Jerry Lewis and Dean Martin, Frankie Avalon, Dick Van Dyke, etc. Elvis was a real hero to us and still is to this day.

After Chico Marx, my second musical influence was the Captain from the Captain and Tennille. He wore that cool, stupid, little sailor captain hat and the '70s teardrop sunglasses; now THAT was cool. Plus, when I saw him on one of those variety show specials he had all those keyboards and synthesizers all stacked up on a stand and I thought that was the coolest thing I'd ever seen. *Love Will Keep Us Together* and *Muskrat Love*, man, those were the kinds of songs that really got me going. I liked all the cheesy guys, like Neil Sedaka, The Carpenters, Andy Williams, and Barry Manilow. I had a real soft spot for sappy love songs and I still do.

I was playing piano professionally by the time I was 13. That meant I'd make some money. It wasn't much, but at least it was better than nothing. I would play little parties, or Bar Mitzvahs, or school plays, or at restaurants or ice cream parlors—anywhere, really, where there was a piano and at least one person and at least a dollar or two to be made. I even had a business card that said, "Cliff Brodsky — Pianist."

I was always a self-starter and little entrepreneur. At first I'd play for a free ice cream sundae, which I considered a great deal because I was gonna play the piano anyway and getting a bonus of an ice cream sundae was great.

Billy McFadden, my basketball friend and neighbor up the street, had his mom give me a crappy little electric piano made by Wurlitzer. It was really old and beat up but it worked well enough to play. And, it was super heavy. Today, those things are considered vintage and not crappy at all. But I guess it was pretty cool and it was portable and even had a little speaker in it. I could take that thing and play in front of people even if there wasn't a piano around.

My first actual paying gig was for Lisa Hirsch's little sister, Audrey's Bat Mitzvah party at the Dartmouth Outing Club on Occum Pond, by the golf course, where lots of events were held. Lets face it: I grew up in a totally utopian, preppy, New England town, with lots of money and beautiful, healthy people.

I had to play "Have Nagila" just once. Then I could just jam on whatever I wanted, noodling around on background music, with little pop/rock/jazz tunes morphing into each other, all the while improvising and making up little sonic vignettes.

I was famous. I had arrived. I was the keyboard guy and the life of the party. Drunk old people would hang out with me and we'd appear to be having involved, detailed conversations while I played and nodded and pretended to listen. They'd make compliments and give me all kinds of attention. I loved that! I was hooked. They may not have known or realized that it was REALLY hard to play the keyboard, listen, and talk back, all at the same time. I guess they were just drunk and lonely and didn't really care if I was listening or not, they just wanted to talk to SOMEONE.

There are a lot of people like that in the world today. Maybe I should be a therapist instead of a keyboard player, it's 99% the same gig.

Quite often a therapist is someone who listens to someone who really needs to talk to someone, anyone, just as

15

long as they are paying attention. So many people are sad because they have so much to say, but no one will listen. Or even worse, if they do find someone who will listen, they'll make that person feel bad for having something to say.

Most people have no clue how to communicate, how to listen, or how to honor other people's feelings. That's why there's so much hate and fear, which ultimately causes war. Most people just don't know how to behave. Period.

My first real steady gig was at Cheese Etc. in the Beer Garden in the back. I was 14 at the time. It was less than a mile away from my house and my step dad would be cool enough to drive me up there, roadie for me (help me carry my VERY HEAVY electric keyboard), and then pick me up at 1 a.m.

They had a little area outside in the back with about 20 tables where the college students would go and drink beers and eat their sandwiches. I used to play there on the weekends, sometimes up to four hours. Some nights I would literally play for four hours without stopping, or maybe only stop once, to eat a free roast beef sandwich, and then get back to work. I was so into playing music that time literally stopped. For me, it wasn't really work. It was my time to learn a bunch of songs, improvising the whole time, morphing between songs and memorizing tunes. It was really the beginning of me getting good really fast.

That place had the BEST roast beef and cheese sandwiches on homemade French rolls—unbelievably good. I had a tip jar on my keyboard and sometimes I'd make $20 in tips alone, and maybe another $40 from the owner. I always got compliments on my playing from the Dartmouth students and locals.

I'd spend time analyzing the crowd and depending on who was there I would think of songs I imagined they'd like. I had already learned a huge, eclectic repertoire of show tunes, jazzy tunes, and mostly tons of pop/rock hits. I'd do my own arrangements and make odd, quirky versions of songs that you wouldn't normally expect from a 14 year-old kid. Like, I'd do a lounge version of "Stairway To Heaven, " just to mess with people and see if they'd notice. Once in a while, someone from the audience would look up, realize what I was doing and either give me a thumbs up sign, or make an acknowledging face that meant they were on to my game. I got really good at reading a crowd.

The owner of Cheese Etc. was this eccentric, crazy lady named Madame Denman. She always yelled at her workers and threw food at them and got all irate and crazy. She had this stoner son named Rob, who used to live upstairs in one of the apartments. He was a good-looking, European kind of dude, with a foreign accent of some kind, probably Danish, or German. He always had a hot chick up there and he always had great pot.

He was such a stoner that he could take six bong hits in one breath. Very impressive. He had a bong that had a gattling bowl on it where you could fill six little one hit chambers that spun on its axis so you could pass it around without having to refill it every time. But he was able to do all six in one breath! I was really pretty impressed that his lungs could handle that much smoke. He was famous in my little pot world of stoner friends for his incredible lung capacity.

Even though I was only 14, I had already been smoking pot for a couple years. It was hard to find, so I couldn't smoke it every day, but I wanted to. I had found the perfect combination that made everything in my tumultuous mind serene: marijuana and music. Certainly not a unique combination by any means, but man oh man, it worked like a charm on me. I would get stoned and play the piano endlessly, getting lost in the melodies and harmonies that would one day turn into a deep love and understanding of music that literally would shape my destiny.

What started out as a way to get attention from the girls (and as a way to show up Alan Breed) ended up being my saving grace. If it weren't for the piano and my love of music – – listening to it, playing it, teaching it, producing it — I don't know where I would've ended up. Probably in jail, or in a psych ward, or maybe in the White House as President of the United States, which in my opinion would be WORSE than jail and a psych ward put together.

The Tree Fort

When I was about 12 years old, the new hockey rink in town was being finished. It took several years, and while it was under construction there was a lot of junk wood lying around that anyone could take. I was amazed by how much mostly good wood there was and anyone with half a brain could build all kinds of cool stuff.

Me and my friend David Skewes figured we'd ask our parents if we could get some and build a tree fort. They said it was fine and we went over there and got a lot of amazing wood that was perfectly good for building a tree fort.

We picked a location with the perfect tree in the back of David's house. It was perfect because it had all the right elements, like the right location with the right branches. We asked David's mom if she would bring

her station wagon to the hockey arena place with all the free wood and she did and we loaded it up, right in broad daylight. It wasn't stealing because it was junk wood. There weren't any signs that said "Don't Take," and no one stopped us, so we figured it was just there for anyone who wanted it. It was a pure goldmine and David and I couldn't believe how lucky we were. David was one of my good friends— for a summer, that is. It seemed in those days I'd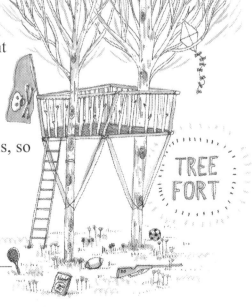

have a best friend for a while and then in about six months I'd either wear them out or they'd bug me and I'd move on. Every year I had a new best friend. I wonder why it was like that. I guess my best friends were seasonal. I suppose I had some long-term friends, so it wasn't like I was a total loser with the friendship thing.

David had a bunch of older siblings and they all turned him onto the cool music of the time. They all had records of bands like *Peter Frampton: Comes Alive, Wings: Band On The Run*, and stuff like that. We used to sit on the floor in the living room and listen to the albums over and over again, just amazed by how good they were. I still remember lying on his living room rug listening to *Blue Bird* by Paul McCartney and Wings...

Anyway, we built a tree house and it was really nice. It was about ten feet high and had a rope ladder hanging down.

David and me used to have BB gun fights in his back yard. One of us would have the gun, and the other would have a metal snow saucer as a shield and we'd basically just try and kill the other guy way across the yard and the other guy would hide his face and torso behind the snow saucer. You could hear the klink klink sound of the BB's hitting the saucer and the occasional "OW!" when a BB would hit someone's arm or leg. I'm surprised we never got one in the eye or got in trouble with his mom. Maybe we timed it so that no one was around when we did that stuff. That summer was a blast. Once the tree fort was up, we probably played in that thing for about ten minutes and then got bored. It wasn't about hanging out in the tree fort; it was about building it. That was the fun part. Once it was up, it was just a stupid tree fort and lost its appeal in about two seconds.

David used to say dumb stuff like, "Hey, you have a pie cost on your shoulder."

I'd say, "What's a pie cost?" and he'd say, "About a dollar fifty," and then laugh and laugh and laugh.

Then he'd say, "Hey, Cliff, you have a hen way on your arm."

I'd say, "What's a hen way?" and he'd say, "About five

pounds," and laugh and laugh. He thought that was pretty clever and so did I, for a while that is. David had an older sister in high school that was pretty hot. She knew I was a musician and would flirt with me some. Of course I would flirt right back. I didn't care if she was five years older than me. She was hot.

He also had an older brother, Johnny, who was into drugs, and in trouble. We NEVER would be like that when we got older, we would tell Mrs. Skewes.

Once in a while, Johnny would show up, but he was mostly "out." When I did see him on his occasional appearances he seemed like a nice guy and a normal enough person. In fact, he was just fine. Mrs. Skewes was the one that wasn't all that fine. She was nice and all, but she was always suspicious of people and just waiting for them to mess up because she basically believed that people eventually let you down. Or, that's what it seemed like to me. Or, maybe I was just learning how to be paranoid and she just happened to be there during that period of my life. I guess I'll never know for sure which came first, the paranoia or Mrs. Skewes being suspicious.

Mr. Skewes was mostly a normal, straight-laced kind of guy. He probably drank alcohol more than the average person, but in my town, everyone drank more than the average person, so even though most people were alcoholics, it SEEMED like it was normal.

I had read somewhere that Dartmouth College had the highest alcohol consumption per capita in the entire United States. Every year, someone in one of the frats would die of alcohol poisoning.

I knew some guys up there and they told me how they'd flood the basement with seven kegs and make the freshmen do alligator slides. They had to run and slide in the beer and drink until they threw up over and over again and then passed out. The older Dartmouth students would stand around dressed in plastic garbage bags, taking notes with a clipboard, making sure the new freshmen guys could aim their

21

puke with deadly accuracy into a big garbage can.

I guess if you're going to be an alcoholic as a profession, you might as well get good at throwing up and aiming it in a garbage can so you keep the mess to a minimum.

The Shack

When I was 13 years old, I started smoking as much pot as I could find. One summer, I was totally against the idea of drugs and the next summer, out of nowhere, it just made a lot of sense. I was a natural at pot smoking and I just loved it. I loved pot more than just about anything, except for the piano. The piano was first and pot was a close second.

David Skewes and I used to get pot from his older brother, Johnny. He was cool. Now that we were pot smokers, we needed to find a safe place to smoke our pot. The tree fort was too much of a bust. It wasn't secluded enough.

I thought that maybe the best thing to do would be to take down the tree house and transfer the wood to my parents backyard because we had a ravine and then a little hill past the ravine and then some woods and a little area that was basically protected and hidden enough on all sides that a cool little fort could be built there.

I asked my parents if David and I could build a little fort in the back and they said fine. So we demolished our tree fort and used the wood to rebuild a bigger and better one behind my house. The only problem was that we needed more wood and stuff. So we went back over to the hockey arena place and scrounged around and got a bunch more wood. We were lucky and resourceful.

This time we'd build a bigger and better fort. This time it wouldn't be a tree fort, but a little shack with a real floor and walls and a roof. A little pot-smoking shack. It would be big enough to hold about four or five people and that was just fine with us.

It was all about finding the right spot with the right tree setup. David and I were good at figuring out these kinds of things. We found four little trees a perfect distance apart that formed a little square, and that's where we attached the beams for the floor. We didn't have to buy one thing. All the wood was free and we had enough nails between our dads' workbenches. It seemed that, where I came from, most dads had workbenches with lots of nails and tools.

It took a good few weeks to build the shack. It was a lot of work and it was fun. We were very focused on our project. Only this time, we didn't bail once it was done. We could smoke pot in there and no one could bust us. We were safe.

For a while, that is.

The shack was basically a Few hundred yards from the Back of our house, definitely far enough away where you couldn't smell anything, which was perfect. It was also about half a mile from the back of the high school and junior high school. It was just far enough away where you couldn't see it through the trees from the school, but you could see the school from the shack. Basically, it was the perfect location for us and all our friends to sneak away from school in between classes, smoke a quick bong hit or doobie, and then run back to school in less than 10 minutes.

It didn't take long for word to get around to the cool people in school. We used to say, "Let's go for a shack attack", which meant, "Let's go sneak off and smoke some weed at the shack and not get busted." It was pure utopia. During the winter, there'd be footprints in the snow from every direction, heading directly to the shack. It was basically the center of the universe.

For a while, that is.

In freshman biology class, I could look out the window and see the shack. It had a yellow plastic tarp on the roof that used to be a two-man tent that David and I put on there to keep out the snow and rain. It worked great, but you could totally see the shack during the winter because all the leaves were gone, along with our protection from being seen.

Our teacher, Mr. Rowe, was a stoner and a super funny guy. We'd say, "Hey, Mr. Rowe, you see that little yellow shack way over there in the woods with the yellow roof?" He'd say, "Yeah, so?" We'd say, "That's where we go every single day before your class to get stoned, right over there." He'd laugh and say, "You guys," and make it look like he thought we were kidding. I'd say, "No, seriously, Mr. Rowe, we get stoned every single day, right before your class, right over there, see," and I'd point and be, like, "Right over there, man, that's where we go."

Mr. Rowe was super cool. He encouraged plagiarism in his class. He flat out would tell us that if we had a paper due on a subject, that it was okay with him if we copied the exact text for a subject, word for word, from the encyclopedia. The reason why he'd let us do that was because the actual act of sitting there and reading and writing EXACTLY the same thing from an encyclopedia was better than not doing any homework at all. He was right, of course.

Our class was Bio-Yellow, which was the class for slow learners, or dummies, or STONERS. Bio-Green was super hard and for all the over achieving kids, the ones who would take pre-calculus at Dartmouth when they were 17 — the smarty pants, show-off types.

But hey, they couldn't play rock 'n' roll on the piano and my life was going somewhere. I was going to be SOMEBODY.

The shack lasted for a few good years until that fateful night of the Frank Zappa concert. The hockey arena was all finished and it was big enough to hold rock concerts. Frank Zappa was on tour and he came to our town, and that night, after the concert, a bunch of drunken older high school kids totally demolished our precious shack. All that was left was the floor.

The next day, me and David Skewes went over there and we couldn't believe our eyes. The wood was scattered all over the place and our precious little shack was no longer. We just looked around in horror at the carnage; all our hard work, all our effort and skillful craftsmanship ruined by a bunch of freaked out Zappa fanatics all amped up from the concert with nothing to do afterwards except crush me and David's private little utopian refuge.

Those weasels! Those rat finks! Those nitwits! What kind of heathen, mongrel, black-hearted vandals would do such a thing? We were so bummed we didn't even care about rebuilding it. The shack was like a one-time thing and it would never be the same again if we fixed it back up. Someone else would just come back and destroy our creation.

There are builders in life and there are destroyers. We were the builders, and they were the destroyers. The hate filled cretins. Our sacred area was tainted and poisoned. The energy there was no longer pure. We must've concluded that the shack was killed prematurely — in the prime of its life — and that it was time to move on. Or, maybe we were too stoned and didn't have the focus or the drive to rebuild it. Or, maybe we were just too depressed to try and even make up our minds how we felt about it.

Let's just say that it was time to move on...

The Diamond Ring

When I was 14 years old, I used to baby-sit to make some extra cash. A lot of families in my neighborhood had me on their list and they'd call me once in a while to see if I was available to basically hang out and watch TV with their kids while they were out partying somewhere. I didn't do infants or any other high-maintenance babysitting. I was more of a little kid sitter and mostly a TV watcher/sitter. I would've been more of a stoned TV watcher/sitter, but quite frankly it wasn't easy finding pot where I grew up. Anyway, I was a great baby sitter.

At this time in my life I was also a kleptomaniac, which meant I couldn't control myself and had to steal. It was a weird condition because mostly I didn't do it to really get anything; it was more like an addiction to adrenalin. I would say I was more of an adrenalin addict than a kleptomaniac, and that stealing was just a subset of the adrenalin activities that I was involved with from time to time.

It wasn't like I was ALWAYS stealing, but I did it enough to qualify as having an actual condition. I suppose if I had tried telling a judge that I wasn't a criminal and that I merely had an infatuation with the chemical buzz from stealing he probably would've told me to shut up and sent me to jail anyways. It's funny how we rationalize things and how our mind plays tricks on ourselves.

Honestly, sometimes it *was* about the stuff. I used to shop lift with some of my derelict friends and we would steal candy and comic books — the usual suspects. A lot of it was about showing off to my loser friends and I have to admit there was a payoff: the rush of stealing is like doing a drug, and of course you get the free candy and what not.

Me and my loser friend Brian Hart snuck into the local theater late one night and stole about five cases of candy. One huge score. The weird thing was, it was pitch black in there and you couldn't even see your hands in front of you. But somehow we managed to find the candy and get it.

Then, while we were carrying the goods, we heard a noise. Someone else was there. It must've been the manager guy who worked there. He didn't have a flashlight, but he was looking for us. I remember distinctly standing in the pitch black of the little area right in front of where you walk into the theater, the area where there are double doors on both sides so as to keep the noise down. Anyway, I'm standing there, scared out of my mind, holding five cases of candy and the guy walks right in front of me, but he can't see me. I had to hold my breath and not make a peep. It was creepy. He was literally two feet away, looking straight at me, but since it was so pitch black I could see him but he couldn't see me. I was invisible. After about two seconds, he turned away and left the premises. That was a close call!

One time, I was babysitting at the Jefferson's, a family up the street I'd known for many years and had babysat for a couple years already. I was snooping around upstairs in Mr. and Mrs. Jefferson's room, looking through her jewelry and found what looked like a fake diamond ring. It didn't look all that great and it was just lying around with a bunch of other fake looking jewelry. I just figured it wasn't worth all that much because it was just sittin' there and wasn't all locked up in a safe or in some fancy jewelry box or anything.

It was just sittin' there, like the ring from *The Lord Of The Rings*, beckoning me, calling to me, "Cliff, go ahead, take me. You know you want to. No one will know. Maybe you could give me to a pretty girl. Maybe I'm real and you can make a lot of easy money off me. Just go for it, man!"

So, I picked it up and took a closer look. I didn't know anything about diamonds or jewelry and still don't, but at the time I knew enough to try and see if it would scratch glass.

I'd heard somewhere that a real diamond was harder than glass and could scratch it. So I tried the dummy's diamond test on the corner of Mrs. Jefferson's mirror and it made a little scratch. Hmmm, I thought, I wonder if it really is a diamond. I just put it in my pocket and forgot about it.

For a while that is...

About two weeks later, my mother came up to me and said, "Hey, Cliff, where'd you get this ring? I found it in your pants pocket when I was doing the laundry."

I just said, "Oh, I don't know, I think I found it on the ground. It's probably fake."

I really had forgotten about taking it and I didn't even try to hide it. I was just a dumb teenager, not really paying attention to certain details, like hiding a diamond that I had stolen. My mother was smarter than the average bear (she used to use goofy little anecdotes like that when I was a kid) and probably had spent some time studying that stupid little ring. She said, "No, I think it's a real diamond. We should take it to a jeweler and get it appraised."

I said, "Cool, let's go see if its worth anything." I wasn't remorseful or worried that I would get in any trouble, whatsoever.

At that time, I was a budding new musician and getting pretty good on the piano. I wanted to buy a Fender Rhodes electric piano and start a rock 'n' roll band but I didn't have enough cash. My step dad said he'd pay for half if I came up with the rest.

Maybe this ring would be worth something like maybe 10,000 dollars, or a million dollars, and then I could buy all kinds of stuff! My mind raced with excitement and anticipation. But I played it cool and pretended to be barely interested.

So, me and my mom went uptown to some jewelry place and the main guy wasn't there but some apprentice-type looking young guy took a look at the diamond and said, "Nope, it's a fake all right. It's a nice one though, probably worth $100 at the most."

My heart sank and I bummed a little bit. My mother said, "Are you sure?" and he said, "Yes ma'am, positive." We walked out of that place and figured it was just as well and that it was no big deal. But as we left, my mother still had a creepy feeling about this ring, that maybe it was real, and maybe that apprentice jewelry bonehead didn't know what he was doing. My mother was no rocket scientist, but she was a little smarter than the average bear. She wanted a second opinion.

We went back to the jewelry store the next day to check again, but this time with the older guy with the big magnifying glass in one eye and the little-hat-and-jewelry-guy outfit. He at least looked the part. Maybe he could tell us if that stupid ring was real or not, so we could get on with our lives. I never once thought about getting caught, or how it must have felt to be Mrs. Jefferson and have her ring stolen. I just didn't know any better at the time. I was like a lot of people who didn't know any better — back then.

The guy took a quick look and nonchalantly said, "Oh, why, yes, that's a real diamond all right. Probably worth three or four thousand dollars, easy." My mother and I looked at each other like, yeah, now we're getting somewhere. I felt all greedy and evil for a little while and just soaked it all up. I didn't feel bad at all for stealing that ring because I'd conned myself into thinking that it wasn't real and was stupid enough to leave it in my pants pocket for my mom to find. I had tricked myself into thinking it was just dumb luck.

It just made sense to say that I found it on the ground. I even made up a little story about how I was pushing our lawnmower up the street to slave and suffer by cutting someone's grass because I was such a hard-working, good little boy.

Not. I was nothing more than a small-time, petty thief, and that's the truth. I feel kind of bad about it now, but back then, for some weird reason, I felt ZERO remorse.

About a year earlier, my first ten-speed bike had been stolen from school. My biological father had given me that bike and it meant more to me than anything in the world. Some rat bastard at school just took it, on the first day of school no less, and ruined my entire reality. It wasn't just a little thing. It was a catastrophic event in my mind and a turning point in my concept of the universe.

What little good was left in my heart was crushed out of existence. I had enough evidence that the world was a bad place, that authority figures couldn't be trusted, that the government was corrupt, that my parents weren't qualified to raise me, and that the history books in school were just made up on the spot half the time.

I wasn't buying any more of what the world was selling. I decided I was at war with the world and would take no prisoners. I had been dealt a lousy hand of cards in the game of life and I was not going to go down with the ship. I'd also determined that the world owed me big time for all the times I'd been victimized, ripped off, cheated and lied to.

So, that's why I convinced myself I had no remorse for stealing Mrs. Jefferson's ring. When me and my mom found out that it was real and worth a few grand, my mom said we had to turn it in to the police because it wasn't ours and it was the right thing to do.

I begged her, "No, please, no, we can't do that. We need that money more than those weasels with their big fat fingers. They're probably bad people and don't deserve this ring." She wasn't buying it and said, "Sorry pal, we're going to the police."

So we shuffled off to the station and told the detective that I had found a diamond ring. I made up a story when and where I had "found" it and they said, "Okay, we'll keep it for safekeeping and if no one files a report in 30 days, you honest, good Samaritans can keep it."

I'd guess the detective knew I had ripped it off but he couldn't say anything because we were returning it under the guise of "finding it." That must've been a little frustrating to that guy I bet.

I prayed that the Jefferson's wouldn't call in to say that their ring had been stolen. Then, I would've been totally busted. I had to keep my story straight or else things would get a little bit sticky. I started to have some mild anxiety attacks, but nothing too serious.

I was sweating it out, for sure, but, believe it or not, I had a lot of experience by this time with intense anxiety. Not imaginary problems, like getting yelled at, but actual, life threatening, dangerous stuff.

I'd been attacked, abused, falsely accused as a small child of stealing and I'd been beaten, tied up, and tortured by my stepbrothers who locked me in a closet and tickled me.

I'd also been blackmailed and forced into all kinds of horrible situations. To me, this ring thing was mildly unpleasant, but I'd been through so much already that I was practically a pro at being in hot water situations. I couldn't tell my mom that I had stolen the ring because once the cops knew about it I'd look like a total loser and get in a lot of trouble. So, I just laid low and hoped for the best.

A couple weeks went by and we got a call from the police. Someone had called in a missing ring and it checked out that the one I had "found" was the one they had "lost."

I guess the Jefferson's were too stupid to suspect that I had stolen it from them and they were just relieved to know that someone had turned it in. Or, maybe they'd reported that someone had stolen the ring and the fact that someone had "found it" and turned it into the police might've confused everyone just enough so that no one put two and two together and realized that I had babysat at the Jefferson's exactly at the time the ring went missing.

I guess the fact that I had spaced and left the ring in my pocket and that a couple weeks went by might have increased the odds of people not keeping track of the timeline. Plus, how can you bust someone who returns a diamond ring into the lost-and-found at the police? It was an unusual case and maybe the cops and the Jefferson's both thought all along that I had stolen it but what could they say?

We gave it back under the condition that we "found it." I was in the clear, sort of, until things got a little strange. First, I got a $100 reward from the Jefferson's. They were so happy that I'd found their ring because it was a family heirloom and worth $10,000. The jewelry guy had lied about its value because he probably would've offered us $800 and we would've taken the money without thinking and he would've sold it to some blue-haired lady for $8,000 or something.

Not only did I get a reward for being such an honest guy, but also word got out to the newspapers. Maybe the Jefferson's called them, or maybe the cops did, who knows, but right after I got my reward, I got a call from the *Valley News*, our local paper. They'd heard that I had turned in an expensive ring and wanted to do a story on me.

A reporter came over the next day and took pictures of me in my tennis shorts, pushing my lawnmower with my big face with braces looking all honest and sincere. It got on the front page and I was a celebrity in my town for a short while.

The article said, "Honest Youth Finds Ring." The story went on and on about how I had found the ring and lost it in the laundry and how my mom found it and how we got it appraised and the whole story. People were coming up to me at the grocery store and shaking my hand and slapping me on the back for being such an upstanding citizen and a shining example of how honesty pays, etc. I felt a little bit like Benedict Arnold. It was getting weird.

Then, it got even weirder.

The article had also mentioned how I wanted to buy a piano and that I couldn't afford to and that I was such a good boy that I would rather turn in an expensive ring than buy my musical instrument.

People were so moved by my story. Little old ladies started mailing me letters with a quarter inside to help me buy my piano. I got letters from priests and church people sending me dollars and checks. They couldn't believe that I was such a good boy and a Good Samaritan and how I had resisted Satan and temptation.

Most people would've probably just kept a diamond ring if they'd found it. I felt like a real ratfink. Just knowing that random people would go out of their way to send me money because of a newspaper story made me feel weird. I had stolen a ring, been caught by my mom, returned it, got a reward, and then I became a local hero in the news! It made my grandiosity with low self-esteem grow exponentially in both directions. How bizarre my life had become. I knew I was on an unusual path, but strange things kept happening to me.

About two years later in high school, I finally got busted for stealing a stereo from a restaurant. I was with my friend, Todd, and I was showing off like usual and we were stoned and sneaking around the building after hours. I figured out a way to get in and we stole the stereo receiver, figuring

34

that we could sell it somewhere for twenty bucks.

The cops busted me because someone had tipped them off. I guess someone overheard me trying to sell it or maybe it was one of my weasel friends that wanted to see me get busted.

It was a fateful moment when my mom answered the phone and she said it was the police and that they knew I was the one that stole the stereo. I was a terrible liar and maybe I just wanted to come clean because my conscience had been bothering me about a lot of other things I had already done. I'd had a good run of about four years of total criminal behavior and had gotten away with all of it. I would sneak into people's homes in the middle of the night and just tiptoe around, like a little burglar nut job. Then I'd see what was in the fridge or maybe make a sandwich and then sneak away.

My mom got off the phone with the police and she knew I was busted. She just knew. I couldn't get out of it. I suppose if I had denied it enough I could've gotten away with it, but the cops made it sound like they had conclusive proof and my mother just looked at me like I was a scumbag and I confessed the whole thing.

I couldn't take being a criminal or being at war with the world anymore. It was too big of a job. It was too hard to keep that hate and fear and anger going.

In a weird way, it was a relief to finally be busted. Living a double life was so exhausting, plus you had to keep track of all the lies and always be ready to bullshit your way out of one more uncomfortable situation. People with A.D.D. make bad criminals.

I had to go to the police department with my step-dad. I was mostly uncomfortable being around him 99% of the time to start with, and we had to sit down together with Detective Gianacolli and tell him what I'd done. It was an extremely uncomfortable situation. I was a tall, skinny, awkward teenager who for many reasons hated authority of all kinds and here I was at the police station again, totally busted.

Detective Giancolli pulled out a list of about 50 unsolved mysteries, from stolen cars to burglaries, including vandalism and all kinds of stuff. He said that I wouldn't get in any more trouble if I confessed to any of those crimes.

I said, "Are you sure? He said, "Positive, 100%, you will not get in any more trouble." I guess he just wanted to check off some unsolved crimes so he wouldn't have to keep wasting his time investigating stuff.

I took a long look at the list and there was a bunch of stuff on there that I had done. I was like, "Yeah, I did that one, and that one, and oh, yeah, that one; uh-huh, that was me on that one too."

I checked off about eight things, from stealing kegs at the Dartmouth frats to breaking into a restaurant, to joyriding in three separate cars, to a couple break-ins. I was a pretty active little criminal in my teens.

The detective kept his word and I didn't get in any more trouble. But I was already in plenty of trouble. In fact, for all I know, he could've totally narked on me and told the juvenile court people everything on the list I had done and they could've all pretended that they didn't know anything and just thrown the book at me and made me do 2,000 hours of service work. I guess I shouldn't have been mad at the police for out foxing me, or the local juvi people for making me do ridiculous punishment work stuff.

Since I wasn't 18 years old nothing went on my adult record, but I had to go to juvenile court and sit in front of a roomful of the town's goodie-goodie parents who were my judges. Some of them were my old Cub Scout leaders, and an old basketball coach's wife, and everyone knew everyone in my town and that just made it worse.

Another day of humiliation and having to sit there with my parents, who were more than pissed at me for all the crap that I had done. They probably weren't mad at me because of how it was going to affect my life, but because it made them look like bad parents. I suppose a lot of folks are like that, but who knows, maybe I was the only one in town who had narcissistic parents.

I probably was just reaching out for attention because I was so desperate for the love that I wasn't getting. That's probably it—I just wanted to be loved. I just wanted to be noticed. Somewhere in my childhood I'd gotten lost in the shuffle and swept under the rug.

My punishment was doing 200 hours of community service. My probation officer asked me if I could do anything special and I said that I could play the piano. She told me that I could choose to work off my hours playing the piano at the old folks home.

I guess it could've been worse. But then again, have you ever been to an old folks home? I had to sit there and play the piano for hours on end with a bunch of old-timers in wheelchairs, all sitting around me in a big room while they complained and wheezed and coughed and scratched and fidgeted and told me about their kidneys failing and how they have gas. It was just about a fate worse than death. But, oddly enough, I knew a lot of old tunes and it was good practice. I had a music book called "Hits of the 90's". The 1890's, that is. Those old tunes were actually pretty fun to play.

Mimi Malcolm, my probation officer, was in her mid 30's and really attractive. She was also one really wise tough cookie. I was supposed to report to her once a week for an hour or so. But after I got to know her, I asked her if it was okay to see her twice a week.

She was the only person in my life that I could actually talk to honestly about what was going on in my inner life, inside my head. She was a very compassionate, wise old soul whototally helped me sort out things that were bothering me and I owe her so much gratitude. During a time when I was just looking for understanding, compassion and love she gave me all of that, and more. Our time together had a profound impact on my life. I never stole another thing after working with her.

Towards the end of our time together, Mimi became ill with cancer. We would meet twice a week, per my request, and she'd be wearing a hat because of the chemotherapy's side effects. Mimi was a guiding star in my life and she was dying and there was nothing anyone could do about it. I'll never understand why it had to happen to her,

What started out as me being a typical common thief, and then getting tons of accolades from the newspaper for being an honest youth, to finally getting busted to meeting Mimi Malcolm and then finally losing her after all that just goes to show that one never knows what's going to happen in life. Those who care to pay attention and notice the subtle workings of the universe will understand that there is divine order in a seemingly chaotic universe.

The Origin of
XORNE

I got my first professional electric piano, a Fender Rhodes, when I was 14 years old. I also bought a little P.A. with the help of my stepfather paying half. Now that I had a real keyboard and a sound system the natural and logical thing to do was to put together a Top 40 party band. So, I asked my friend Mary, who I knew could sing, and of course who I had a mad crush on since kindergarten. She was super popular in school, was good in sports, and was a super achiever, over all. She'd known me since I was six and said she would jam with me. She knew I was the best musician in school.

We started learning Fleetwood Mac songs and Heart songs and Pat Benatar songs. We'd rehearse together after school in the music room, or at my house or at hers. We both had pianos and we spent a lot of time building our repertoire. She and I worked well together and we were both fast learners and naturally talented.

The next step was finding a guitar player. I knew of several older kids in school who could play, so I went to each one to find out if they wanted to join my band. After a while, I found the right guy. He was super good at playing lead guitar and also wrote his own originals and could sing background harmonies.

There weren't any bass players at my school so I asked Andy, my friend from band class, if he would let me teach him the bass. I knew he was a trombone player and musical enough to figure out the bass. I didn't know how to play the bass, but Andy was an intelligent kid and I could teach him the songs from the piano and basically work it out on the spot.

The last instrument was drums and there were a few

guys in school that could play, but the best guy, by far, was Charlie Clouser. He was totally into Led Zeppelin and he could play with that same kind of amazing rock feel. I systematically went out and found the best musicians in school to play with and said "you're in my band now." That's pretty much how it started.

We were rehearsing in my parent's living room after school a couple times a week and we got good really fast. I have to hand it to my parents; they were very supportive and I guess we were good enough that they liked the music. Or, maybe they just figured it was a good way to keep an eye on me and keep me off the streets. Over a short time, our living room started filling up with equipment and speakers and drums and amps and lights and banners and all kinds of music stuff.

We had a decent band, and when it looked like we were actually going to go somewhere we needed a name. We spent a couple days trying to think of stuff and got nowhere. Then Mary, the lead singer, who I was madly in love with, said she was reading a book called *Watership Down* and that there was a word in Rabbit Language called Zorn, that meant destruction.

We thought it was pretty cool. But Charlie, our drummer, insisted that the name had to have an X in it. He didn't carewhat the name was as long as it had an X in it. He was obsessed with the letter X. If our name didn't have an X in it, he might have held his breath until he passed

40

out and turned blue.

We figured that we'd spell the word XORNE and say it meant destruction in rabbit language. We thought it was a cool sounding name even though it really doesn't matter what anyone calls a band, as long as there's a reason behind it. It doesn't really matter what anyone calls anything, as long as there's a good REASON for it.

When people found out about our band the first thing they said was, "what does the name mean?" We had a great explanation and nine times out of 10 people would think it was a pretty clever name.

XORNE got to play some of our high school dances and other schools' dances, too. We knew enough songs to play four 45-minute sets, and then we had some extra jam songs in case we had to keep going. Since Mary was the lead singer we predominantly played female singer songs, like Pat Benatar, Heart, Linda Ronstadt. But some other bands with high vocals like Led Zeppelin also sounded pretty good with a girl singer.

Jon, our guitarist, could sing well enough to do a couple guy songs, plus a couple originals. We were mostly a Top 40, pop/rock cover band, because where I came from that's what everyone wanted to hear.

We actually made $500 a night sometimes! It was really cool to be the center of attention, plus sound good and get paid money, and decent money at that. I guess that's why so many people want to be musicians; it's really a great gig if you can pull it off. It's actually still the coolest job in the world.

During Winter Carnival at our high school, our band wanted to be in talent show, but the judges said that since we got paid we were "professionals" and it wouldn't be fair because we were too good. I guess that was sort of a compliment. They said we could play for fun and so we did and everyone there knew that we would've won the contest because we were easily the best.

41

I sang a song from *Rocky Horror Picture Show*, with just me and my keyboard. It was a pretty risqué song about being a transsexual from Transylvania. *Rocky Horror* was a big hit during those days and I have to admit that it took a lot of balls to do that, all by myself, right in front of the WHOLE SCHOOL!!! I came in second, which was pretty good because I was only a freshman and all the judges were seniors and they couldn't let a freshman win a talent contest; it just wouldn't look right.

That was a great moment I'll never forget; that feeling of doing something totally scary, but doing it anyway, and conquering my fear. Plus, the whole school applauded me and said I was great. That moment cemented in my mind that I wanted to be in show business for life.

I won other talent contests with Mary. One time, we entered a town-wide show and Suzy Chaffee, the pro skier, was one of the judges. Her name was Suzy Chapstick back then because she was famous and used to do those dumb Chapstick commercials on TV.

We did the Fleetwood Mac song "Dreams" and killed it. We knew we were the best in the whole show because it was just plain obvious to me, Mary and everyone else there. We had a great vibe, looked great together and we played great too.

Mary was such a tremendous singer and pretty, too. She was 5'10" with a smokin' body, and long dirty blonde hair, and I was 6'4" and skinny and looked above average, if I don't mind saying so. We would've been a great couple. We had so much in common. She was tall. I was tall. We both played music. Her dad was a history professor at Dartmouth College and so was mine. We both liked to smoke pot and play music and do sports and we were both popular and the youngest kid in a big family. Mary never really wanted to go out with me, but we were great friends and great musical partners.

She was in my class in kindergarten and I had a crush on her way back then. I used to sing to her, *Penny Lane is in my ears and in my eyes...*

Then she'd say, "Oh, that means that you love her" and I'd just drive off on my tricycle, with no hands, and then wipe out and try to get her attention. It was true love for me but she wasn't impressed at all.

Even though Mary and I never really hooked up on the romantic level, we hooked up plenty with music. We had that passion in common and it was probably even more powerful than the man/woman thing, sort of. Plus, we were only kids and not really old enough to be in a relationship. I guess I'll always love her anyway even though she doesn't love me. She was my first love, all the way from kindergarten through senior year in high school. I'll probably be scarred for life over Mary. We sure made great music together, though.

I Dropped Gerber

I've always been a flincher.

If somebody pretended to punch me in the face I would always flinch. I still fall for it. I guess I'm just a flincher. I like that word. Flincher. Flincher flincher flincher. It has a sort of ring to it.

Flincher.

Anyway, speaking of flinching, I was at this high school party one winter, back in the late 80's. It was a typical New England party for me. Basically, somebody's parents were gone, a lot of kids came over and everyone brought their own stubbies. Stubbies were the 12 oz. Bud's and tall boys were 16 oz.

I was a stoner, and just brought some pot, like always. I was never really a drinker, unless there wasn't any pot. Then again, I probably got drunk a few hundred times, mostly in high school, because pot wasn't as easy to get then as it was when I was older.

So, I'm at some girls' house and it's the same old thing: people listening to Lynyrd Skynyrd, the Doobie Brothers, Peter Frampton and Led Zeppelin, playing beer pong, playing quarters, and just hanging out and partying. As usual, the party escalates as the night goes on and everyone gets more and more buzzed.

I'm just hanging out, minding my own business when I see a couple of the more rugged guys getting drunker than the other kids. That usually means sooner or later someone's gonna get dropped by one of them. No one ever really knows who it's gonna be. I didn't really care all that much, as long as it wasn't me, because, like I said, I'm a flincher and not a very good fighter. I was really good at running, though, which can

44

come in handy from time to time.

So I'm hanging out on the stairs that go down to the basement where everyone was playing ping-pong and then here comes Pete Cook and John Gerber. Both played football, both were much bigger and stronger than me, and both were drunk and dangerous. Gerber was so drunk that he fell down the stairs, all the way down, and when he landed he jumped up with a big smile and yelled to the laughing crowd, "See, I didn't even spill my beer!" Everyone cheered. They were quite impressed with his ability for stair acrobatics.

At that moment, Pete Cook saw me and yelled to Gerber, "Waste Brodsky!" Gerber looked at me and without hesitating just started swinging. Since I wasn't drunk, but stoned, my reaction time was quite a bit better than his and I was able to dodge his advance and begin my retreat.

I'm a flincher and a runner, NOT a fighter.

So now, for no reason, I'm being attacked by a drunken, rugged football player named Gerber. I'm in fight-or-flight mode. A second ago, I'm just an innocent bystander, stoned, and hanging out, not causing a problem for anyone. But, since Pete Cook is bored and sees me there, he just figures he'll spice up the party and have Gerber attack me, for no good reason. Kind of like how George Bush attacked Iraq: for no good reason. I guess some things never change. Well, I suppose George Bush had all kinds of reasons; it's just that none of them were the ones he lied to the American people about.

So there I am, running away from Gerber as he chases me throughout the house. Obviously, everyone in the party is watching to see what'll happen while I'm being publicly humiliated, chased, and attacked by a drunken, football-playing asshole. This goes on for a few minutes until he corners me, upstairs in the living room. Gerber's laughing and having a blast while Pete Cook is taunting him to WASTE Brodsky!

I'm completely scared out of my mind and running for

45

my life. I'm trapped with nowhere to run. I'm fucked. I've never been in a fight before. I spent five years in headgear and braces and now he's going to knock out all my perfect teeth and my life will be ruined. All for no good reason. I didn't do anything to deserve this. How unfair life is at times.

We're in the living room with a pretty good-sized crowd watching us. Gerber lunges at me and throws a big, sidearm punch, which I skillfully dodge. I retaliate with two quick, little left-handed rabbit punches, boom boom, and they land square in the middle of his face and his head snaps back just the way you'd imagine a drunk guy's head would snap back when he's getting

rabbit punched in the face. Then I throw a BIG right-handed punch, withnall of the weight from my legs and body and it lands smack dab in the middle of his nose and the POWER of that punch was just like in the movies.

Gerber flies back, and his Legs actually LIFT off the ground and he goes straight down like a lead balloon, crashing on the coffee table and smashing it into splinters.

He's knocked out cold. I feel like a war hero! I've championed the toughest, meanest, drunkest asshole in the party! All the other tough kids from the football team are standing in a big circle around us with their arms folded, smiling and chuckling. It's free entertainment, and they've gotten to see a fun show. One of the kids says to me, "Nice combination."

I'm a super hero now and the toughest guy in the world. It was just like in the movies when someone knocks out someone in a fight, all in slow motion, and they go crashing down onto some furniture splintering it into a million pieces.

The girl who was having the party was yelling at us to

46

get the hell out of her house and that her parents were going to kill her, etc. I didn't care; it wasn't my fault. It was self-defense. I was totally amped up with adrenaline. I was naturally the more skilled and talented fighter and had just defended myself. It really felt unbelievably great.

Now I know why there are wars: it's fun to fight (as long as you win). The high you get from fighting is better than any man-made drug, by far. That's why there'll always be wars. It's a form of addiction and people don't even have a clue about this obvious fact. Not only is it an addiction, its big business. It isn't about religion, or democracy, or defending people from tyrants. War is just stealing and chemical addiction: people get off on hurting other people and taking their stuff. Until we as a civilization get honest with this obvious fact, it will continue, ad infinitum.

Someone from the crowd says, "You have about 15 minutes to get the hell out of here before he wakes up." I guess he'd seen other guys get knocked out and that was the standard amount of time before someone wakes up from being dropped. Now what? I gotta get my stuff and get the hell outta there, that's what.

The next day in school everyone was talking about how Brodsky dropped Gerber at the party. Gerber's face was all swollen and he had a big, fat lip and a bloody nose that was all fucked up. He was ten times stronger than me and a way better fighter — when he was sober.

Now, he was definitely sober and also humiliated and pissed. He was gonna try and get me and it was just a matter of time before he did. But, of course I had fallen into the illusion that I was a war hero and a gladiator and this amazing fighter. I figured I'd just drop him again. I told that to my computer geek, glasses wearing friend, Mike McDonald, who had snot dripping down his nose and unwashed, messy hair, like always. Mike was the smart kid in school and had no

47

friends except the other computer/math geeks who now probably work for Bill Gates and drive Ferraris, while the John Gerber's of the world are busy washing their cars and being called, "boy."

Mike told me that I had better watch out, that Gerber was gonna waste me because everyone knew that Gerber was way tougher than me and that it was just a lucky punch in those circumstances. The bottom line was this: I was stoned and Gerber was drunk, that's the only reason that I won the fight and dropped him — like a lead balloon, I might add. Mike was right, it was just luck and now I was fucked, because sooner or later, Gerber was gonna get me.

I felt a terrible sense of panic but that didn't stop me from bragging about how rugged I was and what a great fighter I was, too. I was gonna milk that situation for as long as I could — until Gerber caught up with me, that is.

I was going over the fight in great detail with some of the guys who saw the whole thing. They were all laughing and saying how great my combination of two quick lefty rabbit punches (technically called "jabs"), and my great right hand, full body punch straight into the middle of Gerber's drunk ass face. It was a glorious story, even though the whole time I was scared out of my mind. But that didn't matter, because the bottom line was this: I dropped Gerber and showed the world that I could defend myself.

I had survived that first day of school after the big fight. I made it home and waited. I knew Gerber was going to try and get me and it didn't take long before he and his friends drove slowly right by my house, making threatening hand gestures like they were all going to wring my neck. I sat in the dining room with my mother, doing my homework and pretending like everything was fine. She had no idea of the things I had to go through while I was in high school. I'd been blackmailed, threatened, jumped, ganged up on, humiliated on a constant basis, attacked numerous times — all kinds of terrible things she had no idea about.

When most people talk about the stress of growing up

in high school they talk about trying to be popular, or getting good grades, or not having zits and pimples. I was dealing with more serious situations, like physical bodily harm, getting busted by police, blackmail, getting narked on — all kinds of things. I had REAL problems.

Anyway, Gerber finally caught up with me, one on one. Just me and him, with no one else around. I had to act fast. I pleaded with him, explaining that I had tried to get away from him at the party and that he had cornered me and there was nothing else I could've done. I told him it was a lucky punch and that everyone knows he's way more rugged than me and that I was a total wimp and not a good fighter. I told him that if he left me alone I would give him a big bag of pot and never mention it again and that he should just be cool and forget the whole thing.

He basically took my bribe and said that if I opened my mouth one more time about how I'd dropped him and what an amazing fighter I was that he was going to personally waste me and that there would be no second chances. I told him that I'd NEVER bring it up again and he left me alone.

I thought that was pretty civilized of him, in a way. Maybe there's still hope for flinchers and civilization as a whole.

Naaaaah.......

Union Village Dam

During the spring of my senior year in high school, some of my friends and me would cut school on a nice, warm sunny day and go skinny dipping up at a secluded water hole at the downstream part of Union Village Dam. All the cool party people knew about U.V.D. because you could go there and drink and smoke and not get in any trouble. You had to walk about a mile through the woods and fields to get there and it was very private. It was great.

Of course, most of the locals knew about it, but it was still a very remote kind of place. It was a cool place to swim, even though the water was too cold for most humans to be in. I hated cold water and still do to this day. I don't even like getting wet most of the time. It's always hardest for me to first get in, but once I do, it's usually okay.

I guess I feel that way about life some of the time.

Another cool thing about U.V.D. (that's what we called it if we were on the phone and didn't want our parents to know what we were talking about) was that the rocks were really smooth and you could slide down the rapids. They were either pretty mellow or bigger and rougher if the dam operators let out more water. You just never knew what the rapids were gonna be like, but you always knew that U.V.D. was a cool place to party.

We used to get our beers from Dan and Whit's Country Store. We'd say, "Let's go get some Stubbies and go party up at U.V.D." or, "lets go to D Dubs and get some Stubs."

One time, a bunch of us were there and we were doing our usual thing: drinking beers, smoking pot and skinny-dipping. Droolson, whose real name was Mike Toolson but he chewed tobacco and drooled a lot so we called him Droolson, was with his girlfriend, Krispy Thompson. Her first name was

Kristy, but she used to party a lot with us and she partied HARD so I called her Krispy because she was frying her brain.

She's all grown up now, married with twins and calls herself Kristen. But she'll always be Krispy Thompson to me. Sometimes she calls me at three in the morning, drunk, and tells me how she misses me and how she should've married me instead of her successful banking-finance-executive-Squares Ville guy.

She pours her little heart out to me in the middle of the night and I keep telling her that if she ever wants to come and visit me that she's invited. But she never does, 'cause in the morning she probably doesn't remember calling me. Poor Krispy Thompson. She's rich, though, and has fake D-cup breasts, but even those don't make her happy.

I've never seen 'em, but she tells me that she's still hot and runs a lot and stays in amazing shape. She was really hot in high school, but always had little A-cup boobies. Not anymore. I bet she's super hot now. There seems to be a trend in America with older women becoming surgically re-designed M.I.L.F.'s.

So, me and Toolson and Krispy Thompson and Goat and Drain Wilmont and Pea-Nut Stone and a few others were down by the river, drinking beers, grinding gears, and dropping queers. That's what the rednecks used to say during holidays when I'd come home from college and see them in the local bars.

I'd say, "Hey man, what are you up to?" They'd say, "grindin' gears, drinkin' beers, bungin' steers, and droppin' queers." I'm not so sure what bungin' steers means, but the rest is pretty self-explanatory.

One of the main rednecks from our town lived right up the street from me when I was growing up. His name was Greg Moulton and he had bright red hair, like all the other kids in his family. He was skinny, ugly, and a real redneck. He ended up being the doorman at one of the bars in town and he'd card all the pinheads.

Pinheads were the Dartmouth students. They called us the Townies. There was a certain rivalry between the Dartmouth Pinheads and the local high school Townies because quite frankly, there wasn't a big difference in size and age.

Greg Moulton would be working the door and carding everyone and finally he got the POWER that he so deserved and had sought after his whole life. He was in charge of the door at 5 Old Nugget Alley and he was prepared to fight to the death if someone tried to pass that door without his permission. He was in charge and he made sure everyone knew it. I guess now I know where those parking lot people come from who will risk their lives in order to get their five dollars or get run over trying.

Back at U.V.D., me and the gang are getting our usual good and drunk and everything's fine.

For a while, that is.

Toolson decides to show off for his girlfriend and do a running, jumping dive into the water. The problem is, some parts of the water are deeper than others. In this case, it's about three

3 inches of water

inches deep and solid rock under that. Unknowingly, Toolson dives in with extra force and when he hits that bedrock with his arm first, something really bad happens. He breaks his arm and the bone sticks right out of his forearm and he's in pretty bad shape.

I'm right there and see the whole thing unfold in slow motion. When the accident happens, Toolson is so embarrassed that he's been stupid enough to dive into a half inch of water that he pretends it didn't happen. He's a little bit in denial. He tells Krispy, and of course she doesn't want anyone to know either because she doesn't want anyone to think that she's stupid for going out with someone so stupid that he'd dive into a half inch of water. So she keeps the charade alive — for a while that is.

Krispy helps him out of the water and instead of screaming and telling everyone that his bone is sticking out, she tries to hide it and makes a little sling for him out of a scarf or something. That works for a little while. But he's losing blood and going white in the face. He's in shock. He's slowly going unconscious and about to die from a lack of blood but mostly, humiliation.

He could fool some of the people, but he can't fool me. No sir—ree.

I casually walk up to Toolson and say, "Hey, man, I saw you dive into that shallow part of the water over there and it seems to me that your arm's broken."

"No, it isn't," he says.

I say, "Yes, it is, I can see your bone sticking out."

Toolson sticks with his story, "No, it isn't, there's nothing wrong with me." Krispy's right by his side and she's sticking with the story that nothing is wrong and that they just don't want anyone to know what's going on.

I said, "I can see it right there. Look. See? Your bone is sticking out right there."

I point to the white part of the bone that's broken and sticking out of his forearm. I mean, like, what could he say to that? He so wants to hide his broken arm, but I pretty much have him busted on that one. I guess his philosophy is he'd rather keep quiet and be thought a fool than to speak and remove all doubt. In this case, I speak for him and bust him.

Denial is not just a river in Egypt.

So, he cops to that fact because he knows he's in

trouble and BUSTED by me, and then I tell everyone what's happening, and we all rally and basically carry him through the fields and woods, uphill, to the main road and call an ambulance and get him to the emergency room.

He probably would've just stayed where he was and bled to death if we hadn't done something. It was odd, dragging Toolson all the way up to the road with a bunch of stoned and drunk guys. Some of the guys that helped us weren't our friends, and in fact were rednecks from a neighboring town we didn't like.

It was really more like they didn't like *us*. But in a real crisis, people band together and do what's necessary. It's kind of like, what if aliens attacked the Earth? We, as a planet, would be forced to cooperate with each other and fight back. Maybe that's the only way this world will ever survive — if we can find a common enemy to keep us focused instead of constantly killing one another.

Not.

The Best Party In The World

By the time I was 18 years old and a senior in high school, I had grown into a six foot, four inch 185-pound big person. My parents would take off for the weekend once in a while and let me pretty much do whatever I wanted. Well, it wasn't so much that they'd let me; I pretty much just did whatever I wanted. I wasn't afraid of them and they couldn't control me. They threatened me with all kinds of things and I was bigger than they were and, I hate to break it to you, but size does matter.

My parents decided to take a weekend off and go to the horse races, one of their favorite pastimes. My step-dad was actually a pretty good gambler and quite often he'd win enough to pay for their whole trip. They told me under no circumstances could I have friends over to our house, or even worse, a party, and I told them not to worry, that they could count on me.

I used to feel bad about lying to my parents when I was younger, but I had learned that telling the truth was stupid, dangerous, and quite frankly, un-American. The second they left, and I mean the actual second; I was on the phone ordering a keg. I could still see the red tail lights from their car driving down our street as I got on the phone with Pat and Tony's General Store and ordered a keg for the huge party I was about to plan. I had no actual plan before my parents left; I just figured I'd begin with a keg and then get on the phone and start inviting literally everyone I knew.

It worked like this. In my very small hometown of Hanover, New Hampshire, when someone's parents went away, they'd have a party and lots of people would show up. In my case, I started calling people around 3 p.m. on a Friday

55

for that same night, and I told them to tell everyone that my parents were gone for the weekend and to invite as many people as they could. I didn't care if my neighbors found out, or if I got caught. I knew I was going to college that fall and would be out of the house soon enough.

Open party at Cliff Brodsky's house; his parents are out of town!

The word caught on like wildfire. I wasn't really all that popular but I was cool enough that the right elements came together allowing a huge party to form. It also could've been that there weren't any other good parties happening that weekend and my timing could've just been dumb luck.

By 5 p.m. I had a bunch of friends over and we were all drinking beers and smoking pot IN THE HOUSE and not worrying about a goddamn thing. We had the whole weekend to do whatever we wanted and by Sunday afternoon we'd clean everything up perfectly and no one would ever know a thing. We got an ice-cold keg up and running. We cranked the tunes, like Led Zeppelin's *Houses of the Holy*. We stayed on the phone taking turns inviting people and they just kept showing up and showing up. It just kept growing. It grew exponentially.

Our house wasn't really all that big, but it was a decent-sized place. You could probably fit 300 people easy in it, plus the backyard and garage could hold another 300. My parents used to throw these amazing New Year's Eve parties with plenty of free booze and probably 500 people showed up at one point or another during the evening.

Once in a while, my parents were cool and that party was a highlight of the year for a lot of people. I sort of took that philosophy of partying and just went for it. I was graduating soon and about to go off to Berklee College of Music in Boston, and since everything was all set, I had a sort of free feeling that nothing could really go wrong.

Well, nothing went wrong that night and plenty of things went right — quite right, I might add. As the multitudes showed up, we kept gathering money and ordering more kegs to be delivered. The beer just kept flowing and more and more people kept showing up. Of course the music was cranking to The Doobie Brothers, or Lynyrd Skynyrd, or *Frampton Comes Alive*, the double album that everyone used to clean their brown pot with.

By about 8 p.m., there were probably 200 people inside, and the party was just getting started. Cars were parked on the side of the street in every direction as far as the eye could see. By midnight there must've been at least 400 people IN the house. They were wall-to-wall in every room, hallway, and bathroom. Every square inch of floor space was filled with people and beer, laughing and joking and partying.

At around 10 p.m., my cool next-door neighbor, Mr. Breed, showed up, holding a martini because he was always up for a good party. He worked for Dartmouth as a fundraiser, which meant he got paid to be a professional partier. Plus, he was my piano teacher's husband and he played the saxophone in a cool jazz band and he was quite excellent.

"Oh, I see you're having a party," he says, and I say, "Oh, its just a little party," and I watch him squeeze through the wall-to-wall people. The house looks completely out of a chaotic movie scene of total pandemonium, literally identical to that movie *Risky Business*, minus the hookers.

The row of cars outside was at least two miles long, and it looked like Woodstock was happening in my house. The Dartmouth hockey coach even showed up! I don't even know how he could've found out that some little shit high school kid was throwing a last-minute party. Pretty much the whole town and college showed up, at some point, during that evening.

Rebecca Baldwin, my neighbor up the street, met her boyfriend Chris Depinto (a cool guy who played rock guitar) at that party and they were making out the whole time in the TV room and I was pretty much the most popular guy in the world that night. I was responsible for creating the environment for young love to happen and that is something of value to some people.

I was hosting a little, last-minute party with just a few friends and it grew into an open party that resembled *Animal House*. It was by far, the best party that I have ever thrown in my entire life. I didn't get laid, or get in a fight or any other type of drama. It was just pure socializing at its finest and I have always loved a good house party where there aren't any uncool parents to RUIN everything.

The funny thing was, the next day, after it was over, it was no big deal. Nothing got broken. Nothing got spilled anywhere, no cops showed up, there weren't any rednecks crashing the party and starting fights. Nothing bad happened and nothing went wrong. It was as if all the stars had aligned themselves in just a certain way where it all just worked out, and everybody had a blast and it was just a pure magical night for all. There was great music, cold beer, good weed, pretty girls, musicians, hockey players, Dartmouth sports coaches, all my friends, plus a lot of NEW friends after that night.

Even my neighbor, Mr. Breed, had a blast; it was cool to see the kids partying with an older "dad" type guy who wasn't giving anyone a hard time and just treating people like human beings, with respect and dignity, and laughing and joking. Plus he probably knew half the people there; my town was so small that most everyone knew one another in some capacity. It was truly a fantastically magical night for all.

When my parents came home on Sunday afternoon, I had already cleaned up the whole place spotless and there was literally zero evidence of any kind of a huge party. It was as if it never happened.

My parents probably knew I had some people over, because they're not stupid, but since I had cleaned up so perfectly, probably even cleaner than it was before they left, they couldn't really say anything and probably didn't even care.

Of course Mr. Breed wouldn't tell on me; he's not stupid either. My parents had a great weekend, I had a blast, and half the town of Hanover N.H. had a wonderful time. No harm, no foul. It all just worked out great.

It was, by far, the best party in the world.

PART TWO

Boston

KILL SLUG

When I first got to Berklee, I always had some sort of moneymaking scheme happening at all times. Piano lessons, music tutoring, renting my sound system, selling weed — you name it; I'd try it to make some extra cash on the side.

During my first semester in the dorms we had this security guard downstairs and he was a pretty good artist. I asked him if he would make me a logo for my new sound company.

CLIFFSOUND.

He drew me a really cool picture of a cliff by the ocean with a cave on top and it had musical notes and a little guitar flying out of the cave. The logo was born! *"Cliffsound: For Sound Ideas"* was conceived!

I had this little sound system that I'd acquired in high school and it was worthy enough to be rented to other Berklee students for little gigs and recitals and what not. Fifty bucks here, 75 bucks there; it was supplemental income. Everyone at school knew who I was, so I always got little gigs and odd little jobs with that sound system. They knew who I was because I went to great lengths to advertise with my cool little logo. I'd make flyers and go around the entire school putting them up on all the bulletin boards. There was another guy in school who had some sound equipment, too, and he was my competition. I would pull his flyers down and he would pull mine down. We were fierce competitors.

One day I approached the guy and asked him if he wanted to join forces and combine our equipment and do bigger gigs. He said why not. Our first gig was at a punk rock club in Boston. This was during the early 80's and punk rock was REAL It wasn't just a thing; it was a lifestyle and people were really into it.

If you really think about it, punk music is mostly about

punk people. A punk person is basically an angry, fear based coward, the kind of person that needs a group to do crazy things with, like Hitler was a punk. George Bush is definitely a punk.

So, we get a job to bring the sound system to this hardcore punk club. Everyone had giant Mohawks and face piercings and combat boots and they all looked tough and mean and angry.

Of course I was wearing a preppy light-blue alligator shirt and Docksider shoes. I completely didn't fit in with that crowd but, hey, I was 6'4 and the sound guy and the punk rocker guys needed a sound system so we HAD to get along. Plus, I imagine the punk rockers LIKE being different, they probably didn't care that I looked like a preppy. As long as my sound system was loud, that's all that really mattered for these people.

Before the bands started, there were some punk beat poets that opened the night. I thought that was pretty curious; I'd never seen a live poet pontificate in public before.

One guy got up on stage and said, very slowly and carefully, "Ronald Reagan, Ronald Reagan, Ronald Reagan." Then he walked off the stage. I guess that was his poem. I thought it was pretty clever. No one applauded, but no one booed either. It was a neutral crowd, I suppose. While watching the beat punk poets I thought I'd also try to write a poem. It took me about 5 seconds and then I wrote this:

The Cold War

Was a cold sore

On the lip of humanity

I thought that it was pretty clever, too.
After the punk poetry people finished, it was time to start the punk rock show. The first band goes on and there's lots of

screaming and people are moshing in the mosh pit. Moshing is basically where people bang and bash into each other in a frenzied dance. Usually some one gets hurt and blood starts flying. I had never seen this before, but in a weird way, I thought it was interesting.

For a while, that is.

Who am I to judge these people? They're punk rockers and that's what they do. I just didn't want our equipment to get messed up. So far, so good. Our PA system was taking the abuse and holding up just fine. For a while, that is. Around midnight everyone is good and drunk and it's time for the main act: KILL SLUG, to go up on stage. I had heard about KILL SLUG and they were supposed to be the meanest, nastiest punk rock group in the area. They were known to start riots and pandemonium wherever they played. I had seen their name spray painted in alleys all over the rock 'n' roll area of Kenmore Square.

I guess the whole punk rock scene was about more than just the high-energy thrash music; it was also the violence, blood and filth that went with the lifestyle. I think the music part of the punk world is just a front for a bunch of assholes to have an excuse to be assholes under the GUISE of it being a cool, artistic statement somehow — kind of like how George Bush is scamming everyone about "Operation Freedom." He should spell it "Operation Free Dumb" because it ain't working over there in Iraq and everyone knows it.

So, now it's time for KILL SLUG to go on stage and everyone is all ready to see a circus freak show. About 300 crazed punkers are all liquored up, drugged on speed, and ready.

KILL SLUG start playing and jumping around and thrashing, like your usual punk rock show. The thing concerning me was, that they start knocking over the mic stands and the monitor speakers, which is NOT OKAY with my new buddy and me.

We jump on stage and put things back in order and then they keep on knocking the equipment over. The speakers were pretty indestructible, but even still, I didn't want my first gig with my new partner to have all our stuff ruined.

No one tried to mess with us while we did our jobs though. I guess they were used to working with sound guys and pretty much didn't care what they were doing because basically punk people don't care about themselves, or anyone else. They just don't care about anything. Not in a carefree way, but in an emotionally frozen, shutdown kind of neurotic way. Its almost like punk rock is a symptom of some form of mental illness.

It was stressful, to say the least. I barely knew my partner and here we were in a highly volatile situation with a lot of angry, drunken, wasted, antisocial crazy people getting off on breaking things and trying to ruin our valuable equipment.

I'm looking at my partner and we're thinking that we gotta get the hell out of there soon before something goes dreadfully wrong. It wasn't about making some extra cash on the side anymore; it was about surviving the night and getting out alive with our equipment in tact.

About halfway through the set, the lead singer pulls out a live chicken and pretends to bite its head off. Very funny, we all think.

Okay, now put the Chicken down, I'm thinking.

Everyone in the crowd is chanting and taunting KILL SLUG to bite the chicken's head off. I can handle a lot of situations, but there are certain things I just can't be around. So the lead singer from KILL SLUG lifts the real chicken over his head and the chicken is trying to get away and it's flapping its wings and feathers are flying all over the place. Everyone in the crowd is mesmerized by the chicken.

The music stops and now it's all about the crazy lead singer with his shirt all torn off, with his tattoos all glistening from his sweat and the lights and this crazy chicken freaking out. The guy has maniacal eyes and is marching all over the stage insinuating that he's gonna do it. Everyone in the crowd is watching his every move and the fever is running high in the punk rock club. He finally grabs the chicken's neck and opens his mouth like he's pretending to bite the chicken's head off and then he really does it! He really bites the head off of this poor, little innocent chicken. The chicken starts running all over the stage with blood flying all over the place and people are throwing up in the crowd and even the hardest core punk rockers are grossed out beyond belief. It was a horrible and disgusting moment!

Enough is enough!
Me and my partner pulled the plug on KILL SLUG and grabbed our equipment as fast as we could and got the hell out of there.

I had never seen anything like that before in my life. It had nothing to do with art and nothing to do with music. It was a freak show and I wanted nothing more to do with that scene. It was the most disgusting thing you can possibly imagine, and if there are any KILL SLUG fans left in this world then you should be ashamed of yourselves and rot in hell.

EMANON

I met Brian Fox in 1982 at Berklee College of Music in Boston. He was a talented and very odd character. We used to smoke a lot of pot together and argue about music. We'd argue about who was the best drummer or what the best guitar solo was or who the best band or producer was. We'd argue about a lot of stupid stuff that was basically nonsense.

Brian was really dirty. Not in the usual sense, but in the general messy sense. He would move into an apartment, never take out the trash and I mean NEVER, until it started piling up. There would be little paths from his bed to the bathroom, to the kitchen, then to his bass and amp. The pile of trash and crap would get higher and higher until it literally became like walking through little paths with walls of mess on each side.

The rest of the place was filled with junk and trash and crap piling up everywhere. He wouldn't do the dishes either. They would just keep piling up and then the science projects would start growing. It was ridiculous how filthy his place was.

It's odd, because he came from a fairly affluent background. He used to tell people that his dad was so rich that he loaned money to banks. In a way, his dad did loan money to banks, but I'm sure it wasn't the way it sounded.

People used to say, "Wow, your dad must be really rich to loan money to banks." Others just scoffed and didn't really believe it because you never could tell when Brian was telling the truth or making things up. I think sometimes he would just make things up to get a reaction from people.

For some reason, Brian and I clicked. Maybe it was all the pot smoking. Or maybe it was because I used to loan him money. (He paid me back, mostly.) Or, maybe it was because I put up with his eccentricities and never judged him. Whatever the case was, we were good friends at first. For some reason, we just got along great. He was a bass player and singer. He also composed a lot of music and had an uncanny ability to do arrangements. He could memorize the most complex forms of music, and the quantity was unbelievable. Of course I would quiz him to see if he was BS-ing me, and he would, without fail, pass my rigorous tests 100% of the time.

His favorite bands were King Crimson, RUSH, and other prog rock bands from the '70s. He told me that when he was a little baby his parents used to play classical music under his crib to help him stop crying. By the time little Brian was three years old, he was playing Mozart and Chopin on the piano, from memory, in the right key. He either was born with perfect pitch or it developed from listening to so much music as a baby.

I had never met a person who had perfect pitch before. I was fascinated by this little trick. I envied and admired him. You could play fifteen notes on a piano, all smooshed together with both hands and he would be able to pick out each note, and tell you precisely what it was. It was truly an amazing talent and had to be seen to be believed. One time, Brian and I were on the subway in Boston and I forget where we were going, but Brian had this really funny face on.

I asked him what he was doing and he said, "Shhhh, I'm concentrating."

I said "What?" and he said, "Shhhh!"

I said, "Wha…?"

"Shhhhh!!!"

He finally told me that an eight-part trumpet octet just formed in his head, from beginning to end. All in a complete thought, an eight-part trumpet octet just popped into his little brain. An eight-part trumpet octet is the equivalent to playing eight separate melodies, at the same time, that don't get in the way and clash. It's next to impossible to do and only the super intelligent can even imagine it, yet write it, in their heads, in perfect pitch. This wasn't normal, I thought to myself.

I, of course, was blown away.

When we got back to our dorms, I took him to a piano and told him to show me his new trumpet octet. He showed me all right. Each part, one at a time, and they all made sense. Basically, it was a modern-day miracle.

Here I was, in the presence of true genius, of a *modern-day* Mozart, and NO ONE cared. That was the weird part. No one gave a rat's ass that Brian could do this. Probably because he was such a pompous ass and a jerk, by nature. He had a lot of antisocial behaviors and was basically an asshole unless he liked you or wanted something from you, or both. He was a jerk, but not stupid. Maybe he was an idiot savant or some kind of offshoot or bizarre experiment gone awry from God. Who knows what Brian was, but he was a genius AND a weirdo. I still liked him, though. I guess I've always been curious about odd types.

At Berklee, during our first year, everyone was required to take certain core classes, like ear training and arranging and harmony. I remember the day when Brian told his teacher that he had perfect pitch and didn't need to do the ear training, that his ears were perfect and that he knew more than anyone at the school, including the teachers, about ALL music.

The teacher wasn't impressed, and in front of the whole class told Brian to prove that he had perfect pitch. The teacher played a note on the piano and Brian said B flat. Then the teacher played another note. F sharp, Brian said. The teacher couldn't believe it and neither could the class.

Then, Brian started to show off.

He said, "Okay, wise ass, now put your whole forearm on a cluster of random notes in a big mess."

No one in the world would be able to pick out those notes or distinguish the exact tones. Brian calmly made his concentrated funny face and listened really hard and then said, B flat, B natural, C, E flat, F, G sharp, etc. He called out each tone and the exact register and all of them were perfectly right.

The teacher just shook his head and said, "Okay, man, you can go. There is nothing that I can teach you. You've been given a gift that transcends this entire school."

No one had ever seen anything like that in the history of Berklee. Maybe in the history of mankind as we know it. It was true. Brian not only had perfect pitch but his hearing was so exact that he could even calibrate an electronic tuning device like a strobe tuner. I guess if you aren't into music this isn't really that big of a deal, but if you are, and truly understand this ability, then it pretty much is a modern-day miracle.

Brian also had close to perfect rhythm. That's a totally different gift and was something he taught himself. He used to sit around with a metronome and try to guess the exact tempo of a certain beat. After years of practicing, I guess he just finally memorized every tempo and was able to tell you the exact tempo of any song, or you could tap out a tempo and he would be able to tell you the exact speed of your tapping. He was a freak and I thought he was pretty clever.

Brian told me that he wanted to start a band and asked me if I wanted to join. I said "sure". I was always up for a good challenge. The problem was that Brian's music was too hard to play. So, no one ever ended up playing it because it was too complicated and precise and exact. But we tried.

For a while, that is.

I remember that somehow I got assigned the tedious and arduous job of having to be the scribe for Brian. He couldn't read music that well because he just memorized everything and did it all by ear. But he had about 60 albums of original music in his head and it was taking up valuable real estate in his brain. He needed me to write down one of the albums, note for note, for his new band.

He called the band EMANON. It spelled the words "No Name" backwards. It was a stupid name, but at least it was a gimmick, of some sorts. He was going to call the band A.C. Fox, which stood for air conditioning, because he thought that was cool.

We would stay up all night, smoking pot and sitting by the piano, and he would sing a note, "Laaaaaaaaaa," and signal for an eighth note, and then I would have to sit there and write down every single little note that he would sing to me. It took us months of staying up all night writing down these ridiculously complex and difficult compositions that would just sit in his head and fester.

I thought it was kind of cool, at first. Like, in that movie *Amadeus.* about Mozart and how the emperor's main composer was all jealous of him and on Mozart's deathbed he would sing notes to the guy from his new Requiem, etc.

That must have been me, in a past life. Because I did it for real in this life and let me tell you, it was an odd thing; to be in the presence of a genius and still have to basically help an idiot who couldn't even read music. After several months, we finished all of the songs. Some of them were seven pages long. We tried to rehearse a couple times, but the music was too hard for all of us. So Brian decided that we should record an album first and then learn the material by ear through the process of recording each part, one at a time.

So we all stupidly agreed to go to Maryland, back to Brian's hometown somewhere, to record at his friend's studio. He had an 8-Track recorder and back in those days that was a big deal. The Beatles only had a 4-track when they started.

The problem at this point was getting the band and all of our stuff to Maryland in the middle of winter. I called my parents and asked them if I could borrow their beat-up, old VW microbus. It was beat up because I was the last kid left in high school and got to drive that van all the time, and I slowly trashed it, fender by fender—little accident by little accident. It still ran pretty well, but there were dents on all sides. Believe it or not, my parents said okay. I guess they didn't really care anymore because the van was pretty much destroyed and they had already moved on to something else.

So, me and Brian and the rest of the band all packed up our instruments and drums and amps and all our crap and drove down to Maryland somewhere. It was like a nine-hour drive from Boston. The problem is, the van didn't have any heat. So we basically were freezing to death the whole time in our winter jackets. To make matters worse, there was some kind of exhaust leak coming directly inside the van, so in order not to die from the poisonous fumes we had to keep all the windows open. Otherwise, we would've all surely died.

It was also 30 below zero, and we had to cruise down in this beat-up van, with a poisonous exhaust leak with all the windows down for NINE STRAIGHT HOURS! Brian threw up about eight times, all over himself, but we somehow made it.

We finally got to Brian's mom's house and she's all mad at us for some reason and yelling at Brian. This, that and the other thing; no one had any idea what the deal was with her. We'd just been through World War III and now we're all getting yelled at by Brian's angry mom. Not a very fun welcome party.

But all of a sudden, Brian's little sister, Jacquelyn, waltzes down the stairs in her little see-through nightie, and she's about 16 and looks like a <u>fully</u>-developed Sophia Loren! I'm like, yeah, this just might work out after all.

It didn't take long for Jackie and me to hook up. Pretty much the next day she and I ended up in her bathtub, naked, and we slept together that night, too. She was so pretty, and incredibly sexy. Her hair was long and dark brown and she had full red lips, kind of like Angelina Jolie lips. She was very thin, but had REALLY nice curves and lets just say that she had been blessed up top.

We didn't have sex, though. We just sort of made out and rolled around. It was more of a fun thing.

The next morning, Brian's mom's boyfriend, Bill, knocked on Jackie's door and just walked right in.

I was like, "Hey, Bill, what's happening?" all smiling and just chilling like it was no big deal. Of course, I got yelled at by Brian's mom, and got kicked out of the house. I couldn't imagine what for. I mean, I was 19 and Jackie was 16 and it seemed perfectly reasonable to me that we should hook up.

The problem was, we weren't trying to hide it and maybe Brian's mom was more bummed because we were so carefree. She probably didn't even really care that we slept together, just that it made her LOOK bad. I'll never know for sure.

But man oh man, was Jackie a stunning young woman with a perfect body. I also heard that she was super smart, but at the time we didn't really get into that.

So me and Brian and the band end up in the recording studio and start to make the record. We were a rag-tag team of misfits and screw-ups, but we were badass musicians and kicked ass at what we did.

We really focused our energy in that little studio and brought all of our handwritten charts and sheet music that I had personally written down, and little by little, the album got made. After it was mixed and finished, we all sat down and went, oh, that's how the music goes. Cool. And it was. It sort of sounded like Yes and Brand X with some King Crimson thrown in. It was a true masterpiece. When it was time to head back to Boston and back to school, the van was still running but the exhaust leak was getting even worse. It smelled like gas everywhere.

One of Brian's stoner friend's was like, "Man, this raggedy old van smells like gas, dude. You should pull over and let me take a look."

So I pulled into a Kmart parking lot somewhere. I was like, "Hey, man, I'm gonna call my dad and ask him what to do." I called home and my mom answered.

I said, "Is Dad there?"

She said, "No."

I told her that the van smelled like gas and I didn't know what to do. She told me I should just figure it out and call her back.

I said, "Okay, I'll just figure it out."

So we popped the hood open and the entire engine was soaked in gas.

Brian's friend was like, "Hey, man, your raggedy ass van is gonna blow up 'cause the engine is soaked in gas and we better do something."

I was like "Yeah, I know. Let's try and trace where the

gas leak is coming from. You stay here and I'll turn on
the van and try to see where the gas is leaking from."

He's like, "Okay, man."

So I jumped in the van and started her up.

BOOM!

The engine area completely burst into flames. We
started
running as the van
quickly became
engulfed in flames!

"She's gonna
blow, run!" Me and
Brian's friend were
sprinting and dove
behind a big trash
dumpster. Nothing
happened. The van
just burned and burned
and burned. No explosion. No nothin'.

Out of nowhere about three minutes later, a big fire
truck came flying by and put the fire out. The van was
completely burned up and totaled. It was amazing how quickly
the entire van had caught on fire. It took about four seconds
before the whole thing was blazing like crazy. I guess vans
don't really blow up when they're on fire; that's just on TV and
in the movies.

So, I looked at my friend, shrugged my shoulders and
then I called my mom back.

"Hey, Mom, guess what?"

"What?" she asked.

"Remember that little gas leak that I couldn't figure out
how to fix?"

"Yes?"

"Well, I figured out where it was coming from and now
the van is totaled 'cause it completely caught on fire and is

completely destroyed. We just got away with our lives, but I'm amazed that it didn't blow up."

She said, "That's just on TV, dumb ass."

I thought I would get totally in trouble for destroying the van but I guess my parents were cooler than I thought, or maybe they were glad to get rid of that raggedy old thing. Or, maybe they thought it was cool that it went out in a blazing fire of glory. They probably didn't think that, but I sure did. There was no mention of us being in danger or potentially getting hurt. I suppose by the time I came along they had already seen enough from my three older brothers that literally nothing phased them. They were broken in.

We borrowed one of Brian's neighbor's vans and drove back to Boston with our new album. EMANON was now ready to rock— and the rest is history.

For a while, that is.

We never really ended up rocking. I suppose the trauma of the long drive down from Boston, and me having an affair with Brian's little sister and then getting busted by his mom kinda made a dent in me and Brian's friendship. We basically were so sick of each other by the time we got back to Boston that we just broke up the band and never got a chance to actually play any of the super-complicated Stravinsky meets Zeppelin songs that I slaved over for months to transcribe and then went through hell and back to record. Just another typical day in the life of some stoner musicians going to Berklee.

Falling In A Pot Hole

I used to love riding my 10-speed bike around Boston. I'd take it down to the Charles River, across the bridge to M.I.T. and further out to Cambridge and Harvard. I'd ride it to Boston Commons and Beacon Hill, down Beacon Street towards Boston University and Kenmore Square. I'd go down to State Street by the combat zone, and look at all the hookers and weirdo's. You name it; I'd been there in Boston.

Since I was stoned quite often, that meant I rode my bike high pretty much
all the time. For the most part that wasn't a big deal. I was good at operating heavy machinery and a 10-speed bike isn't even close to being in that category.

For some reason, I've always been able to function quite well being high except once in a while I'd totally forget where I parked my bike. A few days would go by and I'd wake up in the morning in an absolute panic and realize — yet again — that I had no idea where my bike was parked.

So I'd think to myself, "Oh, no, I've done it again." I'd scramble off to the general vicinity of where I thought I might have left my bike and pray to whatever God I had in my very unspiritual brain at the time that I'd be good and never lose it again, and either it'd be gone, or it was there but all the parts had been stripped.

Usually, it was just plain gone. Once in a while, I'd find it intact and chained to a tree or something else. Those times were lucky. I probably went through four or five bikes that way, which was pretty pathetic, to say the least, and a clear example of how being stoned 98% of the time was really beginning to make an impact on my bicycle riding serenity.

I was 13 when my first 10-speed bike was stolen. My

75

biological father had given me a Huffy for my birthday. It wasn't a great bike, but it was new, and it was mine, and it was from HIM.

It lasted two weeks.

I was an idiot and left it unlocked and someone stole it on the first day of school.

Looking for my bike in a panic and realizing that it was gone, I felt utter terror and hatred and insanity that someone would just do that to me. It was a sinking feeling in my heart and after the initial sadness and confusion and grief I finally came to one stark conclusion: I was finished with the regular world. I was done being a nice, conformist kid that went along with how things were supposed to be. That was the last straw. I was at war, man. I couldn't take it anymore. I was going to start a covert underground army and do everything I could to undermine society, as we knew it. I was going to dedicate every ounce of my strength to creating total anarchy.

I didn't want just one bike thief to suffer, either. I wanted our entire civilization to suffer the pain that I felt that day. When my first 10-speed bike was stolen, it began a regular pattern of antisocial behavior on my part. I can pin it all on that moment in eighth grade. I just snapped. I wasn't going to take it any more.

About five years later, back in Boston, I'm cruising on my sky-blue Bridgestone 10-speed, the crème de la crème of all of the bikes I had ever owned. Since I was good with bikes I had gotten a part-time job at *Community Bike* on Tremont Street so that I'd be able to afford to buy my own, brand new, really nice bike.

So, one day I'm cruising along near downtown Boston on my favorite bike of all time. I was riding in the middle of the street in between some really tall buildings on a typical, busy, bustling day. I was just cruising along, not going that fast, and minding my own damn business. There wasn't too much traffic and everything was just fine. For the moment, that is.

I looked across the street to my left and saw a really pretty girl wearing a tight business suit. I had to turn my head and stare at her great butt. The way she wiggled her ass was straight out of a 1940's movie: the dame with the tight dress and the big ass and skinny little waist and high heels. She looked amazing from the front too; she had long blond hair and was pretty, maybe in her mid twenties, probably going to work with some pep in her step.

I stared just a little bit too long.

My head was turned all the way around, checking out this hot blond babe in the business suit, completely not looking where I was going. I maybe was looking at her three or four seconds, maybe even longer; I don't know, time seemed to stand still, but however long I kept looking was too long.

Crash!

I rode right into a giant hole in the middle of the street! I literally rode straight into a four-foot trench, a massive ditch, completely unaware of the entire thing.

My bike nosedived straight down and I flew off over the handlebars and landed square on my forehead on the concrete. I was completely unprepared for the impact and I totally blacked out. In skateboard terms, it was called a head plant.

I don't know how long I was out cold but I woke up all covered in blood and I didn't know where I was. A traffic cop stood over me, directing cars away from the accident scene and he must've radioed in for an ambulance.

When I came to, the first thing I said was "Is my bike all right?"

The traffic cop just shook his head and said, "Don't worry about your bike. You're goin' to the hospital." He had a really thick, south Boston accent.

I could see the front wheel of my bike practically folded in half. The frame was all bent from the impact and FORCE of how hard I hit that trench. I hit it so hard that it bent a solid reinforced steel alloy bike frame. My favorite 10-speed of all time was totaled.

That was not a good day.

I still have a scar right near my left eyebrow. Guess I was lucky there was a traffic cop nearby; I could've gotten run over by a bus or car or who knows what. Since that day, I have a three-second rule for looking at chicks across the street.

The Giant Sea Rat

During my summers at Berklee College, I used to be a member of the Back Bay Boathouse. It was loads of fun going down to the Charles River and sailing in those cute little Mercuries and 470's. They were small boats, but could hold four or five people no problem.

I was a pretty good sailor and would go at least two or three times a week for an hour or two. I had learned how to sail in summer camp when I was a kid back in New Hampshire, plus we'd sail on other occasions on Sunfish and Sailfish boats. Suffice to say, that by the time I got to the Back Bay Boathouse I already knew a lot about sailing.

I could hop on my bike and be there in ten or fifteen minutes tops. It was very relaxing and almost therapeutic in a way, to go down there and sign up for a boat and then set up all the sails and rigging and all that sailing stuff. It was a fun little ritual, for sure.

Right after my second semester at Berklee, I found a couple guys to team up with so we could move out of the dorms and find a cool apartment. I picked a Chinese punk rocker and a Latvian pianist. We were new friends but became pretty tight as the months went by.

We all put on our best suits and went to an upscale real estate firm in the Back Bay of Boston. They only dealt in high-end properties. We found a young realtor agent guy who had a nice suit on and he liked us right away.

We all lied about what we did for a living. Of course we didn't tell him we were music students at Berklee. That would've been stupid and guaranteed that we wouldn't find a cool pad. So I said that I was a famous record producer and my Chinese buddy said he owned a restaurant and my Latvian friend said he worked as a recording engineer at Synchro

Sound on Newbury Street. That was the recording studio where The Cars made all their hit albums.

Actually, my buddy did work there, but as a runner; he got them food and cleaned up. Our little charade worked, and the realtor guy told us that there was this amazing three-bedroom apartment on Marlborough Street in the heart of the trendiest and best part of the Back Bay. He said it was going to go condo, but that it might take a year or two or three. We didn't care; we were living for the moment. Six months would've been cool enough. He told us that we could live there for HALF PRICE because it was a time sensitive issue.

Our new best friend, Mr. Realtor guy, showed us the apartment, which was unbelievably nice. It was on the third floor of a brownstone building with an elevator that went right to our front door. The apartment was a floor through, meaning that it ran from the front to the back of the whole building.

A beautiful three bedroom, three bath, with a nice big living room and central heat and a/c with a nice modern kitchen. It had real bay windows that you could sit and watch the pretty girls down below and it even had a rooftop area where you could throw fun parties for the building.

It was by far, the coolest, and best apartment I had ever seen in my whole life. Certainly for Berklee standards it was the Taj Mahal, by far. Our realtor told us that it was going for $1,500 a month, but because he liked us and probably knew that we were bullshitters (but somehow respected that), he said he'd give it to us for $750! That meant it was only $250 a month for each of us to live there! We couldn't believe our good fortune, because it was such a killer pad, and the neighborhood was incredible and the whole arrangement was just pure magic. So we pretended to be cool and said that we needed to talk about it first and then get back to him. After about 30 seconds we said we'd take it.

Let me tell you about my Chinese punk rocker roommate. He had one of those rock 'n' roll haircuts that was kind of like spiked, but long in the back. Sort of a punk mullet;

a munklet!

He was from New York City and played rock guitar. He sort of acted like a tough guy, and wore sleeveless cut away sweatshirts, with the punk rock hair do and the spiked leather wrist bracelets. He actually wasn't that great of a guitar player and barely could understand music, but he was a cool guy and a pretty good cook. I guess his parents owned a Chinese restaurant in New York and he used to make us one of my favorite dishes: baked chicken thighs and legs with BBQ sauce, white rice, and frozen corn. It may not sound that exotic, but when you're a 19 year-old college kid, it was pretty darn good.

I told him about how much fun it was to go sailing and he said he had always wanted to go, but that no one ever gets to go sailing in New York City. He had a thick New York accent and you could tell that he was a city kid and probably had never seen much of anything except a lot of big city stuff, which, if you ask me, isn't really all that much. It's a lot of garbage and rats and angry, pushy people with a lot of tall buildings and concrete everywhere. Don't get me wrong. New York has a vibe, and it's cool and all, but it's also a really dirty, rotten, filthy place with too many self-centered, mean people.

One day, I asked my punk rocker roomie if he wanted to go sailing, and he says, "Yeah, sure, I'll go sailing. Are you any good?"

I say I'm the best and he has NOTHING to worry about. He'd never been on a sailboat and even though he claimed to be a tough guy from N.Y.C., he was obviously a little scared about going sailing. Even tough guys who can't swim can drown — just like that.

We went down to the boathouse and signed in and got our little life preservers and got ready to go sailing into the sunset. The area of the Charles River that we could sail around was between two bridges and probably wasn't more than a mile long by a half-mile wide, at the most. But it was enough to get a good little sail in, for sure.

Our Mullet wearing rocker was all excited and acted like a little kid, all laughing and joking and smoking his cigarettes and being all cocky and confident with his thick New York accent. Little did he know what was in store. He was saying how he wasn't afraid of anything and how sailing was for sissies and that even though he didn't know how to swim it was going to be a piece of cake.

So, we're cruising along kinda slow and not much is happening. Sometimes, the wind on the Charles River is kinda not very strong but it picks up the further out you get. My buddy starts to get a little bored and he's like, "Hey, man, can't you make this thing go any faster?"

I look at him with a dull, Garfield-like glare and don't say anything.

He's already acting ungrateful and annoying me, and I feel like pushing him overboard. Anyway, out of nowhere the wind picks up a little and the boat starts to tilt and I tell him to hang on and LEAN back.

He starts to get all scared and like, "Hey, man, can you slow this thing down a little?"

I'm just ignoring him at this point and doing my own thing and telling him to hang on tight and lean back, but don't fall in. I'm the captain of this ship and he's going to have to just take orders from now on, simple as that.

So we're cruising along and after about 20 minutes we get near the far end of our little sailing area by the bridge and we notice an odd thing. There's this funny looking whirlpool spinning around slowly and gurgling with bubbles and stuff.

My buddy points it out and says, "What the hell is that?"

I say, "I dunno, let's take a closer look, shall we, and see for ourselves?"

All of a sudden, my friend is getting kind of white in the face and starting to panic a little, with his little punk mullet fluttering around in the wind.

He says, "I don't think that's a good idea; we better stay away from that thing."

I, of course, ignore him, and head STRAIGHT for the whirlpool. I'd been over that little whirlpool a thousand times and knew that it was just an underwater drainage thing and that it was harmless. But it did look kind of scary to the uninitiated eye.

We arrived at the murky whirlpool and now my crew of one is out of his mind with fear.

"I gotta get out of here, man. What the hell is that? I've never seen anything like that in my entire life!"

I tell him with a straight face while I'm looking directly into his beady, little, scared Chinese eyes that a giant sea rat lives under there.

He looks at me with the most scared Chinese punk rocker mullet hair cut white face and says, "The what?!! A giant sea rat! Are you kiddin' me?"

I'm like, "No, man, for real."

He's crazy now with fear — completely beside himself.

"A giant sea rat! What the hell are we doing here? How could I have been so stupid to let you take me here!!"

I tell him, "Listen, man, there's a six-foot, man-eating giant sea rat under there and you better be cool because he attacked some sailors last week and drowned three of them." I said it really seriously.

"What the hell...we gotta get outta here, there's a giant sea rat down there, man!!! I knew we shouldn't a gone sailing...get me outta here, man!!!"

I guess when you're from New York City you see big rats all the time and maybe a giant sea rat really isn't that far of a leap when you've never been sailing before — and of course, if you're not that bright.

OOH, That Is Some OTHER Shit

I knew this guy at Berklee who was my black friend. We used to smoke a lot of pot, listen to jazz, and play chess. A lot of chess. He was tall and good-looking and always had a white girl with him, or he was about to hook up with one.

I guess he liked white girls. I like white girls, too. Anyway, he was a character and I liked him. (Not in THAT way, but in a normal, healthy way.) His name was Albert Sutherland, I used to call him Al, and I think he was from the Midwest somewhere, like Missouri or something.

Al had a funny saying he'd always say, over and over, but in different ways. He would normally say his funny saying when we were listening to jazz music. The saying was, "Ooh, that is some other shit." I cracked up every single time he said it. Every single time. He liked that I Always cracked up, so he kept saying it different ways, kind of like how a jazz musician would approach it.

There are pretty much infinite ways to say "Ooh, that is some other shit." You could say "Ooh, that is some OTHER shit," or "Ooh, THAT is some other shit," or "Ooh, that is SOME other shit..." It was all about what accents on which

85

words and the subtle inflections on the rhythm of the phrase. Arn would usually say his saying when we were stoned and listening to Joe Pass, Larry Carlton, John Coltrane, or Oscar Peterson. We would hear something and Arnold would say, "That is some OTHER shit."

After a while, I started saying, "That is some other shit," and he cracked up because I'm the white guy trying to sound black and he thought it must've been cute or something that I was imitating him. The thing was, though, that I wasn't really trying to imitate him. When I really thought in the moment that something was some other shit, I would say that because I meant it. His saying was infectious.

Al also used to hook me up with good pot deals. He was sort of a small-time pot dealer on the side. We were pretty tight, and I used to consider him a pretty good friend. We spent a lot of time together. We must've played at least 500 games of chess. He was actually a little bit better than I was and reminded me that he was on the chess team in high school. That impressed me. The bottom line was, he could beat me more often than not, and I am no slouch at chess, so I thought it was pretty cool that he was that clever.

But he wasn't that great of a musician. He practiced and practiced guitar all day long, or so it seemed. Even so, his chops were kinda too fast and way too sloppy. He never just played anything cool; he always was trying to reach a plateau that he couldn't quite maintain. I know a lot of people who play like that and if they could just play within their means, then they would be fine. Maybe someone should just say something sometime and clue these people in. Maybe someday I'll just say, "Listen man, play within your means, because that ain't happenin' like that." But hey, I'm just one guy and it's only my opinion, (even though I'm right on this one.) Albert should have been on talk radio, doing something else besides music, because he was so good at saying that dumb phrase over and over in a million different styles. In a way, his musical creativity was being channeled into that funny saying and not into his guitar.

One day, while Al and I were friends, he asked me if he could borrow a 10-speed bike. I used to work at a bicycle store and I convinced my boss that Al was cool and that he just needed to borrow the bike for a couple days. So we lent Al a really nice bike and that was cool. For a while, that is.

Albert never gave it back and it made me look like a real jerk. After that, he basically disappeared. The guys at the store warned me that it sounded fishy and that I better be sure I could trust him. I told them that he was different and a really good guy.

I couldn't believe that he would do that to me, after all that fun we'd had and all those good times of hanging out playing chess and listening to some really great bebop and jazz and commenting over and over in all different ways "that it was some other shit."

I'd see Albert around once in a while after that episode and I would say, "Hey, man, did you return the bike yet?" He'd say that he was going to do that tomorrow, but he never did.

I quit my job at the bike shop soon after in disgrace, and Albert and I never really hung out all that much anymore. I guess he was just a thief and I was just a sucker for his "other shit" charm. He's probably still saying "Ooh, that is some other shit" to some knucklehead in St. Louis somewhere, riding that stupid bike as a homeless, chess playing, bad jazz musician...

Every now and then I'll say "that is some other shit" to an old friend of mine who went to Berklee because he knew Albert and that famous saying; but it's just not the same without Al being there, laughing with us and saying in his own special way, "Ooh, that is some other shit."

Jumped

I was walking home from a party, by myself, at 3 am. I lived on a street that was next to a really rough neighborhood. I had NO city street smarts and shouldn't have been walking that late, by myself, in that area of Boston. Plus, being slightly buzzed from the party I was a sitting duck.

I had $400 cash on me in my back pocket because I was going to buy a quarter-pound of pot, but the deal had fallen through so I had a nice little wad of cash on me. So there I am, walking alone on a dark street next to a bad neighborhood all buzzed with a pile of cash on me. Gee, I wonder what might happen next...

Out of nowhere, three black guys jumped out from behind a parked car and whipped out a knife. I could see it glistening from the street light directly above us.

The first guy, who was the leader and in front of the other two guys lagging, said, "I'm going to kill you," and without hesitation, I gave him the finger, said "Fuck you!" and turned and ran as fast as I could.

Unfortunately for me, it was winter and the sidewalks were all slippery with black ice and I was wearing Docksider boat shoes, which are probably the worst shoes in the world to run in. I'm sure my worthy adversaries had the latest in basketball shoes or some kind of running shoes because (let's just be honest) street thugs may not be the brightest kids on the block but they're at least smart enough to wear good sneakers, just in case they need to chase someone or run from the cops.

So, one second I'm walking home from a party, whistling a happy little tune and minding my own business, and out of nowhere three street thugs with knives jump out from another dimension, threaten me and start chasing me.

I instantly change my course of action. I'm running and slipping and trying to get away as fast as I can and it won't be long before they're all caught up and can stab me in the back while I'm running.

I think to myself, do I really want to have on my gravestone, "Cliff got stabbed in the back while running away?"

No, I'd rather have it say, "Cliff got stabbed in the chest REPEATEDLY and BRUTALLY by a GANG OF THUGS while fighting to the death with every ounce of his strength until he bled to death on the street."

It never once occurs to me to just stop running, hold up my hands and say, "Okay guys, here, take my $400." I'm running to avoid having my money stolen. I'm running because it's the first thing that entered my mind when they pulled out their weapons and threatened my life. You could call it a classic case of fight-or-flight response, an innate, survival mechanism implanted in my reptilian brain from millions of years of evolution that figured the odds would be better if I just got the hell out of there really fast and asked questions later.

After about eight more very long seconds of running and thinking, I stop. I'm done running. I turn, crouch down real low and scream a death cry at the top of my vocally trained lungs.

"MOTHERFUCKERS!!!!!!!!!!!!!!"

I can hear my voice echoing off the buildings. It's the loudest, scariest and meanest sound I've ever made in my 20 years of life on planet Earth. It's the kind of death cry early man might have made while being chased by saber-toothed tigers or a gang of cavemen with rocks.

Most people have never experienced this kind of situation. They may have read about it, or watched it on TV or at the movies. Not me. I lived it. I was prepared to fight to the death by ripping their throats out with my teeth and clawing their eyeballs out of their face with my fingers. I was ready to fight back like a wild man out of control, if that's what it would take to save myself because my life is definitely more valuable than all three of those scum bags combined.

I would've taken one of them and put their face on the curb, opened his mouth and jumped on the back of his head, breaking all his teeth and his jaw and permanently fucking him up for life. I was determined to take a couple of them out with me if it was the last thing I'd ever do.

I wasn't afraid to die anymore. They knew it and I knew it, and they knew I knew it. I'd be damned if my gravestone would read, "Cliff was a coward." Not me. I may be a lot of things, but I ain't no coward.

I was all crouched down real low so whoever got to me first was going to have me spring up at them with all the force coming from my legs and I was going to go straight for their throats with my teeth and fingernails and try to kill the closest one as fast and efficiently as possible and worry about the other two later. I heard somewhere that if you're outnumbered the best thing to do is to attack the meanest one as hard as you can and take them out as quickly as possible — something about group dynamics and the rest of the gang either respecting you or fearing you.

I'll bet that while these guys were chasing me, they

were doing some thinking, too, like, "Shit, usually people just get all scared and give us their wallet right away without any trouble." Or, "Man, this guy looked like he was gay or something and an easy target, but now he's all freaked out and pumped up and he's acting all crazy and he wants to fight us all to the death; what a drag."

Or, maybe they weren't thinking anything, like a school of sharks on autopilot, just cruising the black waters at night. Who knows what the hell they were thinking? In that moment, I couldn't have given a rat's ass what was on their minds.

After I screamed "Motherfuckers!" I couldn't believe what happened next. They just froze. It was as if they hit an invisible force field surrounding my body. Maybe their reptilian brain recognized that death cry as a very serious sound that's only made by people who are ready to die. It's a sound that very few people have lived to tell about, because they're usually killed.

In that moment, time had frozen solid. They couldn't move, I couldn't move; I had run and turned to fight to the death. Let's just say for theatrical purposes, it was a tense moment.

I don't really know what happened next because I was in an altered state of consciousness, but I could have sworn I heard someone from behind me yell something. Then, for no good reason, they just turned and ran away. I couldn't believe it. I looked around and there wasn't anyone anywhere. There wasn't anyone behind me or up in a building somewhere. I was all alone, under a street lamp, in the middle of the cold, wintry night. I wasn't dead, or even wounded. What the hell had just happened? Why did they just give up like that and run away? Someone up there must really like me.

I jumped out into the middle of the street, where I could see more clearly my surroundings, in case anyone else was hiding behind a car again. There was nothing. No nothin' no place. They had totally disappeared. It was as if they jumped

91

out from another dimension and then jumped back through a wormhole back to their world. Not a trace of them could be found. I scanned my surroundings and saw some lights coming from a *Store 24* down the street a little ways. I was all pumped up beyond belief and ran down the street towards the lights into the all-night convenience store. I told the guy at the counter that I had just been jumped by three black guys with knives and got away. He didn't say anything or care; probably had been there for years and seen it all.

I don't remember what happened after that. I guess I just called a taxi and went home. But I've thought about what must have happened and how I was able to get out of that situation. It could have been a few different things. It could have been the fact that I gave their leader the finger first, said "Fuck You!" and ran right off the bat and that might have thrown them off a little and rattled their little pea brains some. They might've figured I was just too much trouble and not a quick and easy target. They probably were just looking for some quick cash and too lazy to have to actually fight for it.

Or maybe other people that they had mugged had given up so easily that they were spoiled and used to people just OFFERING them their wallets and watches. Not me, man. The first thing I did was give them the finger. Everyone knows what that means; it doesn't take a rocket scientist to figure that one out. I wasn't just going to offer them whatever they wanted just because they pulled a knife on me. I may have been from a small town with no street smarts hardly at all, but something inside of me knew what to do and I didn't need an Ivy League education to know how to handle this situation.

Or, maybe what happened was that after I screamed at them and then turned to fight they might have realized that I was 6'4", and not such an easy target. Or maybe they thought that I was on some sort of freaked-out drugs like crystal meth or crack and that they didn't want to deal with a crazy white boy.

Or possibly it was my Native American belief that we all walk with animal totems, sort of like animal spirits and that when we are dealt with a life-and-death situation, an actual, for real life-and-death situation, they come out and protect us. Maybe those three motherfuckers saw a real tiger or black bear or bison or wooly mammoth spirit energy field standing side by side with me. I bet that's what probably happened.

Or, maybe some guy down the street or up in a building really did hear me scream and had yelled something back and they just figured the jig was up, that there element of surprise was over and that they better split.

But, my guess is that they just knew that it was going to be a big crazy fight and they were going to get seriously injured and that I was crazy and bigger than they thought and just too much trouble. I guess mugger's work on the art of surprise and this situation had turned on THEM. They must have figured that they should retreat and could find a much easier and simpler target.

I'll never know for sure what really saved me on that fateful night or why it happened to me. I just know that I have faced a life and death situation that most people will never experience. Even if I could've turned back time and avoided this scenario or erased it from ever happening, I wouldn't have. This experience unlocked in me an ancient survival mechanism that is still alive and well. I have been tested, as if I've been in some kind of initiation rights with a secret group of elite warriors and ancient wise men of days gone by.

I will spend the rest of my life unafraid to die, and know, to my innermost self, that I am protected by invisible forces that have proven to me that I'm on this planet for a reason and that I have purpose.

Capsized:
A Sailing Incident

It was so windy down by the Back Bay Boathouse that there were hardly any sailors out on the river. The water was really rough and there were big white caps. Probably too windy to be sailing with little boats, but not so bad that the expert sailors couldn't handle it.

I certainly figured I could handle it, I mean, it was just a little river with little waves, how bad could it be? They used different flags for different weather conditions. This particular day was a red flag day. My kind of a day.

Anyway, I think my rating wasn't high enough to go out by myself, so I had to find someone to go with me. It didn't matter if the person knew how to sail; I just needed some extra ballast, (that's sailing talk for extra weight). I started looking to see if anyone was around and there weren't really that many people there, so I went back to the park area in front of the boathouse to find someone to take sailing.

I finally found someone that I could ask; I saw this really pretty girl in her early twenties sitting there reading or something. Somehow, I seemed to have this sort of radar for certain types of people. I don't know why, but I was always able to find cute, single girls, who were just sitting there, minding their own business. So, I just walked up to her and made pleasant conversation for a few minutes, like, "So, what are you reading?" — that kind of stuff.

We hit it off well enough and then I asked her, "Hey, do you wanna go sailing? I'm an expert sailor and you will have a blast." She sort of hesitated and didn't really know if she should, plus she didn't know me from a hole in the wall. I don't think she wanted to go, but I kept telling her how much fun it was going to be and how it was time in her life to go on adventures and be swept away by knights in shining armor. In my case, it was more like preppy guy with alligator shirt.

She fell for my enthusiasm and, finally, after enough of me trying to convince her, she broke down and said "OK". I told her not to worry and that there was nothing to it and that I never have crashed or tipped over or anything like that. I told her that it was a no-brainer basically and that she could trust me and that everything was going to be fine.

We walked over to the boathouse and signed in and picked up our life vests. I had my new sailing partner and we were all set. It was REALLY windy out, but I figured it would be really fun, and I knew for sure that we were in no danger. I had sailed on that little river for over two years and at least a hundred times, and I was for all practical purposes a bona fide expert. So we got in the boat and put on our little life vests and set sail.

The wind was really gusty and in a few seconds we were flying. My new sailing friend looked like she was having fun, and I said, "Hang on, we're going for it!"

Everything was fine for a while and it was a total blast. I taught her how to lean back and which ropes to pull and how to come about and duck your head so you don't get hit while the boom swings across the boat. I showed her how the rudder and tiller worked and about the tell tales and about how different angles achieved different results with speed. I told her about port and starboard and used fancy nautical terms like beam reaching and luffing. She was very impressed. I was the captain and she was my crew. We both knew our roles and it was a simple plan to understand.

I noticed there weren't any other boats on the river and I thought that was odd because it was in the middle of the day and it didn't really seem all that windy. Just because it was a red flag day and just because the waves were really high and crashing all over the front of the boat and were white caps, that didn't really phase me much. Remember, I was an expert sailor and this was a piece of cake.

About ten minutes into our sailing expedition, a giant gust of wind came out of nowhere and tipped us over. It all seemed to happen in slow motion because I could feel the immense power of that wind and we both were leaning really far over the edge of the boat to try and keep it from tipping over. But the wind was easily ten times stronger than we were and it had a mind of its own. I should've let go of the main sail but the wind just came out of nowhere and caught me by surprise. We were no match for the wind that day and we just tipped over into the rough, red flag day water of the Charles River.

The water was super Rough and it felt like we were in the middle of the ocean. One second everything was cool and then in an instant we were

thrown into the water and bobbing up and down trying to hold on to the side of the boat. It was always like that for me in life; one second I'm good and then out of nowhere I'm thrown into a situation that I have no idea where it came from or how to deal with it and it usually was totally embarrassing.

Unfortunately for me, these little boats were just a bit too big to stand on the centerboard and right them back up. At least if that were the case, I could have gotten us out that jam and even though we were totally soaked, at least I could have solved the problem somewhat. In this particular case, if you tip over with this particular sailboat, you also start to capsize and completely turn bottom up. That's what happened, and now there I was, with this soaking wet chick I barely knew, hanging on for dear life.

It was like one of those scenes in *I Love Lucy* where she was in a crazy situation and it kept getting worse and she couldn't get out of it. It was one of those scenes in life where you really just wanted to sneak away without anyone noticing. But I couldn't. I was stuck with this perfect stranger who just glared at me like I was a total idiot. I bet she couldn't believe she was stranded in this upside-down boat in the middle of total storm conditions on the Charles River.

I felt like a total loser and totally embarrassed, once again. This feeling was not new to me and even though it happened to me MANY times before, it still never got easy to get used to. It was a terrible, completely lame feeling of just being in the wrong place at the wrong time with the wrong person and not being able to quickly make an escape. It was an elongated temporary moment of complete bumming with no relief in sight.

I just looked at her and half smiled and shrugged my shoulders and was like, "Hey, this never happens. I'm so sorry. I can't believe this. I don't know what to tell you."

It was a total catastrophe and, not only that, we had to sit there in the middle of the Charles River for about half an hour, soaking wet, with all our clothes on, clinging to the side of the wet, cold, dirty, stinky boat, until the stupid rescue guys figured out that we had tipped over and finally showed up to get us out of that stupid river.

She wouldn't even look at me, and I was in one of those places in life where I just had to let it pass as soon as I could. I had to take the uncomfortable silence and grin and bear it. She was so mad at me and rightly so. It was all my fault. I had pulled her out of her little comfort zone. She'd taken a chance on a total stranger, and within ten minutes our lives had been literally turned upside down.

Finally, the rescue guys saw that we were upside down and they sent out the rescue team in their fast little speedboat.

They threw us a line for me to tie to the handle on the bow so that they could tow it in. Then we climbed into the rescue team motorboat and they zipped us back to the dock. This poor girl was so bummed at me for ruining her whole day, and she was kind of a shy, quiet type, so she couldn't really yell at me and get it out of her system.

There was a big sign in the office of the boathouse that said basically that they were not liable for any accidents and that you had to agree to sail at your own risk.

As we were leaving, I sort of pointed towards the sign and half smiled and put up my hands like, "Hey, the sign says right there that you gotta take your chances when it comes to sailing here"...she just looked at me like I was a total loser and stormed out of there while her sneakers were making that squishy sound shoes make when they're filled up with water.

I yelled over to her when she was about 50 feet away and said, "so does this mean that we have to stop seeing each other?"

The Tubes, Todd and Utopia

I first heard about The Tubes from my friend Vic Luke back in 1984. I had heard about The Tubes from other people here and there, but Vic was the one who really got me started. He went on and on about how great they were and went into great detail about their awesome drummer and singers and the guitar players and the keyboard players and how great the songs were and the stage show, etc.

Vic was a big fan. He'd go on and on about the show and the hot back up chick singers, and all the costume changes of the lead singer. So, I was pretty intrigued and it sounded like a pretty cool band.

Vic told me that The Tubes were coming to Boston and that there was free outdoor concert at M.I.T. and that we should all go and check it out. It sounded like a good idea and, hey, why not? I was in college and it was the 80's, and it was fun to be a college kid in Boston.

We all went to check out The Tubes and when we got there it looked like a pretty cool setup. It was a free, outdoor show in front of some frat at M.I.T. They were smart kids over at a completely different breed of people than the college I went to. Musicians aren't like the average M.I.T. student. But, I didn't feel intimidated because, overall, musicians were cooler than M.I.T. people, and I was there to check out the music and, of course, the chicks. That was a given.

At Berklee College of Music, there were about 6,000 guys and it seemed like only about 15 girls. The ratio was not good. Of the 15 girls, about half were gay. The others were either ugly or taken. So, I didn't get a whole lot of girl action at my college. I had to go to other schools to find the fine women. This particular time at M.I.T. was primarily about the music, but if there were hot chicks, that would be fun too. I had to go to B.U. or Emerson or Tufts or Northeastern to meet the single, straight women.

The stage was fairly elaborate and I was a total equipment geek, so I was checking out all the amps and keyboards and guitars and all their cool stuff. The P.A. was really big and powerful and super high quality, so I knew it had the potential of sounding really good. I had been to concerts and shows before, but I was never really completely blown away by anything that I'd seen in the past. I was excited to see what The Tubes were all about because I had heard so much about them from Vic Luke.

When they started playing, I immediately noticed that they were better than any other band or show that I'd ever seen in my entire life. It only took about 15 seconds and I knew I was in the presence of something really great. Everything about The Tubes was super great.

The drummer was, and still is, a super monster player and by far one of the best funk rock drummers who ever lived. The bass player was totally a pro and locked in with the drummer, and it was obvious that they had been playing together for years because the chemistry between them was unmistakably tight.

There were two guitar players and two keyboard players, plus two backup singer/dancer chicks who were totally hot. The lead singer had it all: a super great voice, charisma, stage presence, a great personality: everything you could ever want. Plus, the actual songs and music were by far superior to anything I'd ever heard live. These guys were real good and I mean, they could play. Not only was the band great and the material really well crafted, but the physical sound quality was also out of this world. It was clear to me that the sound guy had been mixing these guys for years or he was just incredibly good.

I was blown away. I am not blown away easily. I have a very critical and discriminating ear and little to no tolerance for mediocrity. This was my first experience of seeing one of the best bands of all time, live, with an amazing sound system and everything working perfectly. It was from this moment on that I gained a new level of expectation about what a great live band should sound like and be like. It was proof that it could be done and that there was enough technology and skill and talent to make something like that happen, in real time, in the real world.

The Tubes were so good that I was literally mesmerized by the whole experience. My life would become different. The molecular structure in every fiber of my being had been altered, bringing me to a new level of consciousness. (I don't say that lightly, either.)

It wasn't so much that their message was all that spiritual or that I was so moved by how amazing they all were as human beings. I was amazed at how fuckin' good this rock 'n' roll band sounded on EVERY level. I had never seen people able to play so well and sound so good, all at the same time, and with such a good sound system. That made all the difference in the world. It was a perfect mix and I mean perfect. Plus, every single member of the band had a great voice and could play and sing at the same time and it was a perfect blend. They all had unique and interesting voices and the quality of the sound was just so right on.

The Tubes were truly a great band and the songwriting and arranging was outstanding. The show was a flawless mix of great songs, amazing singing, amazing playing, and an awesome sound system. Everything was flat out amazing. I'm still amazed just thinking about it right now.   I was now a Tubes fan and they were the best live band that I had ever seen so far in my life.

For a while that is.

Until that one fateful night, when everything changed.

I went to see the Tubes again when their *Love Bomb* tour came to Boston in the summer of 1985. Some random band that I had never heard of was opening up for them. When I got to the show, my nerdy friend from Berklee (whom I can't even remember his name) was telling me about the opening act.

He told me it was Todd Rundgren's band, Utopia.

I was like, who's that?

He couldn't believe that I had never heard of Todd Rundgren and Utopia.

Sorry, dude, but I don't know who they are.

He went on and on about how much of a genius Todd was and how great Utopia was, etc.—blah blah blah. My friend was kind of a geek, so I didn't believe a word he said. I was there to see The Tubes, my favorite band in the whole world, and I wasn't about to get all excited about some random opening act that NOBODY had ever heard of except for my random skinny-ass friend who I don't even remember his name right now.

So, the lights dimmed down low and the band walked out on stage. They were all wearing white jumpsuits and had wireless mics attached to their lapels and they were using instruments that were also wireless. There were no amps or monitors on stage and it looked totally barren and naked. I guess the monitors were under the stage through the metal grills or something.

The fact that there was NOTHING on stage except four guys and their instruments seemed a bit odd, but I was mildly interested to see if they could pull this off. The drummer had an interesting drum set that was on a revolving pedestal, positioned so that it looked like it was a motorcycle. It was kinda cool in a stupid way.

The first song started and I was instantly surprised by the playing, singing and overall vibe. I turned to my skinny, white trash know-it-all friend, what's his name, and said, "man, these guys are really good. It must be just a lucky break or something; otherwise, I would've heard about these guys before."

My loser friend just shook his head like I didn't know what I was talking about and told me to shut up and listen. I did, and the band just got better and better every second as I was listening to them. I was truly amazed that these four guys were all singing in four-part harmony, and playing intricate and difficult musical parts that all worked perfectly for the pop/rock genre they were pulling off. It was even kind of a progressive rock-pop sound and it almost reminded me of The Beatles but it was more intense and more complicated.

It was almost as if it were what The Beatles would have sounded like if they had stuck together longer and could play, sing and write BETTER. This was better than The Beatles. I was, and still am, a ridiculously huge Beatles fan, but in all honesty this was ten times better — more interesting, better playing, better sounding — just better. Not better looking though, I might add. This was not about looks. The Beatles were way cooler looking.

I was becoming more and more amazed as this was happening. It wasn't just better songs, better playing and better sound. The actual arrangement and specific chord choices and specific chord voicings and inversions that they were choosing to use were all better, too. It was all so tasteful and master-crafted and intelligent and honest and legitimate and basically perfect. It was SUDDENLY my favorite kind of music in the whole world, and I never knew who they were or where they came from.

I thought that this can't be and that it must be just a lucky first song and that there is no way that anyone could be this good without me already knowing about it. The second song kicked in and a different guy in the band sang lead. They all took turns singing lead. No one hardly ever does that. It's a very rare thing to have more than one lead singer in a band. I had never heard of such a thing or ever saw anything like it before.

The second song was even better than the first. Now, I'm getting weirded out by the fact that a band that was this good had gone totally unnoticed by me and unannounced to a lot of the world. How could a band this good go so completely unnoticed in the world and be opening for a fairly small-time band like The Tubes? Why weren't these guys huge? Why weren't these guys super famous like Aerosmith or The Beach Boys or U2?

This was the best band in the world by far, in every possible way! It had the best songs, the best singing, the best playing, the best arrangements and the best sound. The only thing it didn't have was the show. It didn't look amazing. It was just great music, without an amazing visual made just for a guy like me.

The third song started and it was yet another guy in the band singing lead. There were four lead singers and they all took turns singing lead and backups for each other. My friend sitting next to me told me it was Todd Rundgren's band and that he was the leader. I just was so amazed that I had never heard of these guys or this guy Todd.

From that moment on, my life was different.

I had decided that I wanted to find out who this Todd Rundgren was, and learn how to be like him, in certain ways. Obviously, I didn't want to be exactly like him; that would've been crazy. But musically speaking, this guy and his music hit a nerve in me that no one had ever hit quite like that before.

I mean, I would say that The Beatles were the most successful pop rock band that ever was, by far. I would say that Led Zeppelin was the best hard rock band that ever was. I would say that Elvis was the best male singer/performer that ever lived. Then, I'd say that there are a lot of other truly great singers and songwriters and bands out there and that I had a lot of other favorites, like Freddy Mercury and David Bowie and Stevie Wonder.

But, to be honest, this Todd Rundgren and his band Utopia was in its own world class with me. After seeing Utopia perform that night I had made a new commitment to music and to excellence. I had seen it demonstrated to me, personally, right in front of my musically trained ears, with no smoke or mirrors. It was raw talent and skill and expertise in the field of live musicianship and it was the real thing. The molecular structure of my D.N.A. and my entire reality about what music was, had been uplifted to a new height. I had seen my favorite kind of music for the first time and it blew my mind.

I was also a huge jazz fan. Oscar Peterson was by far my favorite jazz pianist. The thing about jazz, for me, was that it was just too hard to play really well. For me, that is. I guess some people had more of a knack for it, or maybe they worked harder than me. Who knows? I just like pop music the best to play; it makes the most sense to me.

Todd's band, Utopia, made the most sense to me that night. It was very specific, too, the way the upper structure triads in the guitar and keyboards worked with the sophisticated, modern bass lines that weren't playing obvious clichés where you had to really pay attention to figure out the harmonic progressions.

I had studied harmonic ear training at Berklee and excelled at being able to hear the most complex and difficult chord progressions, but these...these were like no other that I'd ever heard before.

It was like hearing all my favorite sounds and colors of harmony that I never knew I loved so much, for the first time, right in front of my face, over and over again. I'm not going to say it was better than sex, but it was better in a different kind of way that stimulated a part of my brain and soul that has never happened again. Not like this.

After the show, I came home and started my research on Todd and Utopia. I found out a lot of things about who he was and what he had done. He was a multi-instrumentalist; he could play the shit out of the piano, guitar, drums, and horns, and sing his ass off, too. He also was a successful record producer and had produced artists/bands like: Cheap Trick, Meatloaf, XTC, The Tubes, Hall and Oates, and many others. His resume was very impressive and his skills were beyond belief.

I have spent 22 years studying him in great detail and have come to this conclusion: he may be my favorite overall musician, artist, producer and performer, but he isn't my favorite human being. I don't know him personally, and it really doesn't matter to me if I do or not. I just can tell that he isn't as amazing of a person as he is a creative force and innovative artist.

I can separate the two things. Just like with Elvis. He is my favorite male performer, but I know for a fact that he isn't my favorite human being. I know it's a strange thing to have such affectation and extreme interest in a musical performer, but not really care about them much as a person. Most people like the musician AND the music at the same time. I do too, quite often, but not in this particular case.

I had heard a sound on that fateful night, showing me it was possible to be that good. Not just that good, but a very specific sound that would shape the next 20 years of my life on a very specific and focused journey towards discovering my own creativity and inner voice. Todd Rundgren and his band Utopia influenced my own song writing and production style more than anyone else, by far.

PART THREE

Hollywood

The Drive To Hollywood

Right after I graduated college it was time to move to Hollywood. I picked Hollywood because I'd learned there are only four places on earth to be if you want to make it in the music business: London, New York, Nashville, or Hollywood.

I didn't want to deal with London. New York was too scary and dirty and Nashville had too many rednecks. I'd already done the redneck thing and I wanted a big change. Hollywood was the place for me. Hot chicks, lots of good weed, the sunshine, and rock n roll, baby! It just made a lot of sense to me at the time. It still does, for different reasons, of course.

My parents gave me $1,500 for graduation, just enough to buy a beat-up, raggedy old van to get me cross-country. I guess I have some kind of weird karma with raggedy old vans. I found this Ford van for $1,500 from some farmer dude in the boonies. I went over there to check it out and the van was in pretty decent shape, certainly good enough to make it to Hollywood from the east coast.

The guy who sold me the van was Paul Travis. He used to use the van to take his family camping. He was a Christian and I guess they were a Christian Camping Family. The funny thing about this van was that the bumper on the front was missing and Paul Travis had finagled on a wooden bumper. I took a closer look and read the words TRAVIS TRIBE. They were etched into the bumper, except the letters were backwards, so I guess if you saw it in your rear view mirror you could read it, or, maybe it was because if you crashed into someone you'd leave an imprint of your name. That's probably why he did that.

So I bought the Christian-Camping-Family-Travis-

Tribe raggedy old van and got ready to move to Hollywood.

Everything was all set to move with my friend, Kyle. We were good buddies in college and had already planned on moving to Hollywood together. Kyle had already stored some of his stuff in my parents' garage and it was all set. He was even with me when I bought the Travis Tribe van.

But on the day of graduation, Kyle gave the commencement speaker a music demo that he made in MY studio, not to mention for free. It turns out that our commencement speaker was a famous record producer. So, the next day this famous producer guy called Kyle and said he was blown away, etc., by his tape, yadda yadda yadda and Kyle moved to New York instead of L.A. and made tons of cash singing, etc.

I was left totally on my own. I've always been a loner and a self-starter, so that was nothing really new.

I packed up my van with the help of my step-dad. He was the kind of guy that prided himself on his uncanny ability to be able to determine which shapes fit best with other shapes and literally packed to the brim every available square molecule of space in the van. It was completely filled with all my recording equipment and furniture and had just enough room for me to sit in the driver's seat and drive. I joined Triple-A and got a bunch of free maps and then I got a little credit card from my hometown bank in case of emergencies. Finally, it was time to head out to Hollywood in my raggedy old van packed to the brim with all my crap.

It was June and just a month after graduation. In my family, after high school, you either get a job or go to college. I went to college and stayed there for as long as I could. I even took some courses twice, just so I could avoid the harsh reality of surviving in the real world 'cause I had no clue how to do that.

Anyway, I found myself in my van, all packed and ready to go and saying goodbye to my mom and step-dad. The problem was, that two weeks before, I flew out to Hollywood to find an apartment. No big deal, right? Well, I had borrowed a Ford Escort from one of my old roommates and was sitting at a traffic light when, all of a sudden, Bam! Some asshole crashed into us at 60 miles an hour! Me and my friend, Jim, and some runaway singer/songwriter that we found, got the world's WORST whiplash!

I mean, this was no joke. It was unbelievable how bad that accident was. It STILL hurts right now, 21 years later! Her car got totaled and we all ended up with neck braces, with permanently damaged spines.

The accident was by far the worst one I had ever been in. It was incredible, because the guy that hit us was in a Toyota Celica, or something like that, with the big black rubber bumpers that are perfect for ramming into someone at a stoplight. There wasn't one SCRATCH on that Toyota, and the whole back end of that piece of crap Ford Escort was all crimped in like an accordion. Just like in the cartoons, except this was real!

After we got crashed into I jumped out of the car to see what the hell had happened. I was in shock and not aware of the PAIN that would eventually plague me for the rest of my natural life.

The runaway kid we had picked up hitch hiking looked around the inside of the car, panicked, then jumped out and ran away without looking back. Maybe he didn't want to deal with the cops or who knows? I still remember one of the melodies that the little runaway wrote, called, "Lovely Little Henrietta" and the hook was, "Lovely little Henrietta, we can leave this town together..." He wrote catchy tunes for sure.

Anyway, I got out of the car and I'm looking at the accident, trying to sum up the situation, and the guy that crashed into us slowly backs up and I'm shaking my head like, no way man, you are NOT going to split from this accident scene.

The guy tries to leave, but I jump in front of his car and slap the hood really hard and yell, "you aren't going anywhere dude!" The guy just stops, locks his car, and sort of freaks out and we all wait for the cops to show up.

Eventually they come, and I explain what's happened and the cops take a look at the guy's car behind us and there's literally not even a molecule size scratch. There wasn't even a speck of dust that had rubbed off that super strong Toyota bumper.

I'm thinking to myself, "man, Toyota sure makes some super hard, indestructible bumpers."

The guy claims that he didn't crash into us, and the cops LET HIM GO! Can you believe that shit? So much for our police department, who are supposed to serve and protect. I don't think so. These guys were so stupid they couldn't have even sold ice to an Eskimo.

The day after the gnarly whiplash accident I called my friend Brian who had moved to Hollywood already and I told him what happened. He said his drummer, Snare Baby, knew a place for us to go to get our necks fixed. When I woke up the next day it was so bad I couldn't even lift my head from my pillow. It was like my head had been cut off, and was just connected by a thread.

Snare Baby's mom was a Scientologist and she worked for some crackpot chiropractors in Hollywood. Snare Baby told me they all specialized in working on necks from car accidents and we didn't have to pay because it was a rear end accident and we had the right insurance and our case was really good.

The chiropractors were all connected with the right Scientologist lawyers and basically scammed the system and us by "taking care of us." Basically, most doctors and insurance companies and lawyers have a little game they play when it comes to rear end accidents. It's not just Scientologists that play this scam.

In those days, the only kind of people I trusted were guys with names like Snare Baby, Furry George, Table Salt

111

Johnson and Crossy Kitten. Last I heard, Snare Baby blew his head off with a shotgun. The way they found him was, his neighbors SMELLED him after he was already dead for two weeks. Nasty.

Anyway, Scientology is nothing more than a science fiction con that destroys peoples' lives and permanently damages unsuspecting naive victims. It's a cult and it's all 100% nonsense. It's dangerous and a huge scam on an international level.

But, the bottom line was this: those weirdo's did a great job with my neck and got me a pretty decent settlement through their shyster lawyers. They may be naïve, crazy, cult members, but they aren't stupid.

I guess a lot of people are like that. Or, maybe a lot of people are crazy, naïve, and are being scammed, but still manage to get some things done.

So, two weeks later, I'm back east, wearing a neck brace and I can't move my head ONE INCH, and I'm not exaggerating. I literally had the world's worst whiplash injury and all the muscles in my neck were torn to shreds and it literally hurt to walk or even BE in any moving vehicle, let alone attempting to drive one.

The pain was totally unbearable for any ride in a car of five minutes or longer. But I found myself driving alone in a neck brace, on a 3,000-mile journey, in a vehicle with bad shocks, a crappy AM radio, and no air conditioning.

But, hey, it's rock n roll man, I'm saying to myself, and I'm going to Hollywood to make it! Nothing's gonna stop me. Think of all the people who have made the perilous journey across the country and survived, like Lewis and Clark. Or, what about crossing the country in covered wagons and being attacked by Indians? I was on an adventure and I was gonna make it and nothing was gonna stop me, man!

So, I got in my van, turned my ENTIRE body in the direction of my parents and waved goodbye to them by lifting

ONE of my arms very
CAREFULLY

so as not to cause
a JOLT of
PAIN
to
go

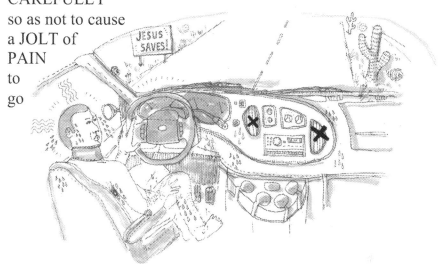

SEARING through
my shoulder and neck and I FORCED up a big smile and off I
went.

I made it out of the drive way and realized that I
couldn't even turn my head far enough to say goodbye and that
I was in total pain and it had only been about 30 seconds since
I'd left!

But I was young man, and I could do anything. Or so it
seemed at the time... Somehow, I made it to Texas after a
couple days of agony and it was in the middle of June and
there was nothing on the radio except bad Bible belt religious
crazy people talking about Jesus or bad country music singing
and strumming about Jesus.

I was totally dying of heat and had no air conditioning.
I was in severe pain the whole time and was sitting there in my
underwear and a neck brace listening to bad Jesus music going
over bumpy roads with bad shocks going, "ouch, ouch, ouch,"
the whole entire way...it was not pretty, and I wouldn't wish
that experience on my worst enemy.

Of course, the van broke down and overheated and, of
course, I managed to find some redneck mechanic to take out
the thermostat and get me back on the road. As I approached

southern California it was like that scene in Midnight Cowboy, where Joe Buck (played by John Voight), had his little radio on the bus and he was heading for New York City and WABC is playing and he's all excited and laughing and smiling, telling everyone on the bus that he's going to New York City and that he's gonna be a hustler and take over that town in two weeks!

That's how I felt as I approached the Los Angeles basin…like Joe Buck.

Yippee! I thought to myself. I'm gonna make it in Hollywood and show the world who I really am. It won't take long either, no sirree, not long at all before I become a VERY famous musician. It'll be easy.

I finally made it to Hollywood — after seven days in total on the road in my raggedy ass van in my neck brace with bad shocks, wearing just my underwear cause the A.C. died around Amarillo Texas.

I have arrived in Hollywood!

Things are gonna be different now, man. Just wait 'til they discover me, and all my amazing talents. It shouldn't take long, either. It'll just be plain obvious to everyone that I'm the next big thing.

I've been telling everyone I know since I was 13 that I was going to be a millionaire and the next big music sensation and that it was just a matter of time. Just a matter of time really, that's all it's gonna take…

I wonder how I survived driving across the country under less than ideal circumstances. Maybe it's because I have a certain destiny. Or maybe it's just in my blood.

I heard that my grandfather drove to the Seattle World's Fair in the 50's on a motorcycle, all by himself. But see back in those days the darn motorcycles weren't really designed for long-distance travel. So, by the time he got there, all the extraneous parts had vibrated off. All that was really left was just the wheels, the motor and a couple other odds and ends.

He must've just held on to that old raggedy ass motorcycle, vibrating his face off with that determined look he always had. He wore those old-fashioned goggles with a leather helmet from World War I and a big scarf. He must've just held on to that giant vibrator and through sheer determination and willpower he made it all the way across the country. Maybe I get my tenacity from my crazy old grandfather. Who knows for sure why people do what they do?

Riff Mic Stand

When I first got to LA in 1987 I had a girlfriend named Nina. Her mom worked in the advertising department at a Jewish newspaper and got me a free ad. I advertised for Piano and Voice Lessons — first lesson free. I only got one call. It was from Riff Mic Stand. It's true; his name really and truly was Riff Mic Stand. Or, at least that's what he called himself.

Riff came over to my apartment in Hollywood for his first-lesson-free deal. Little did I know that my life would never be the same.

For the worse, that is.

Riff came over, wearing black leather pants, a black t-shirt, a black leather jacket, and a headband (a very '80s look I might add). He had beady little ratfink eyes and a big, Jewish nose. I later found out his real name was Mark Lemming and that he would troll up and down Hollywood Boulevard, slingin' his acoustic guitar and singing poorly written songs out of pitch. He really was just a high-pressure phone sales creep from Bumfuck, America with less than no talent.

I shook his hand and said, "Nice to meet you Riff. Come on in and let's get started with your first free voice lesson."

He was a real piece of work, but you know Hollywood, it's the weirdo epicenter of the world with more per square mile than any other place on earth. I figured I'd give it a shot with Riff Mic Stand, and after our first free lesson, I thought I could make a couple bucks showing him how to sing some songs and maybe play some stuff on the piano, here and there.

Riff started telling me he was going to be the best *rasper* who ever lived. I later found out from Riff's twisted mind that a rasper is someone who sings with a raspy voice, like Bonnie Tyler, Joe Cocker or Janis Joplin. He said he wanted to walk down the street and have people go, "There's

116

Riff Mic Stand, he's the best rasper who ever lived."

He wanted people to call him a "Bitch." He said his favorite song was Bonnie Tyler's *Total Eclipse of the Heart.* So he started singin' it right there.

"Turn around, every now and then I get a little bit..." and I stopped him a second and I said, "Hang on Riff, let me close my windows so we don't disturb my neighbors." The real reason was because he was so tone deaf, and so horribly terrible that I didn't want my neighbors to complain and get me kicked out for attempting to teach an insane Hollywood Boulevard freak with bulged out, Marty Feldman eyes how to sing on pitch! Listening to this off-pitch, eccentric-beyond-belief, no talent of a schmuck nitwit gave me monumental physical pain in my ears and a terrible spiritual pain in my soul.

Once we got started I said, "Okay, Riff, let's do some scales.

"La la la la LLLAAAHHHH…"

He was so bad, so friggin crappy that it made my very sensitive little ears start to feel really awful. I graduated Berklee College of Music in Boston and was a trained, professional musician! Ear training and many other highly developed skills were part of my core curriculum so to sit there and listen to such a nightmarish wacko was just too much to take!

I said calmly to Riff, "Hey listen man, I'll be right back, I have to go do something in the back room, hang on a sec." So I sprinted into my bedroom and screamed into a pillow as hard as I could, because listening to Riff Mic Stand attempt to sing was so deafeningly painful that I just about almost lost my mind! It was *that* bad; I mean it, man, this guy was by far the biggest freak I had ever met in my entire life!

I came back from my little scream fest feeling a little bit better. So I said in my best attempt at faking a calm tone, "Okay, Riff, now let's try it again."

This insanity went on for about another half hour and

then Riff said, "Thanks for the FREE voice lesson."

He might have been insane, but he wasn't stupid. In fact, he was just smart enough to be dangerous. (There's a fine line between insanity and idiocy.) The only real reason that I didn't just tell Riff to walk out my door and never return was that I had this fascination with odd characters. I have since learned to have more discretion when it came to picking new clients, but at the time I hadn't yet learned that lesson. I guess you could say that my people picker was broken. I think a lot of people have broken people pickers. Like maybe Peter Piper picked a peck of broken people pickers…

Unfortunately, Riff continued to study music with me and I was stuck with him for a while. During his lessons, I had a few conversations with him and he told me some pretty bizarre stuff.

One time, he was telling me a little about his life and he said that he was a *great* football star back in high school. He'd tell me all about his glory days as the football star who saved the big game and how much of a local hero he was.

He went on and on about how great he was and that he was really a **tough** guy. He bragged about how he was a member of the Jewish Defense League and that he was by nature a very non-violent person, but if you ever, and he said EVER, wanted to fight him then you would be sorry. He showed me how quick he was and did a series of rabbit punches in the air really fast like a total spazz. I guess that was to show me that he could punch really fast, like in cartoons or something, and that I was supposed to be somehow impressed. I just went along with it to humor him; I knew I was in the presence of an escaped mental patient.

Actually, I was mildly amused by his ridiculous behavior and I needed the money, so I sort of had to trick myself into being nice.

I was like, "Wow, you must be a really good fighter, I'll certainly make sure that I never piss you off."

118

Riff had this really annoying whiny, Ratzo Rizzo nagging sort of voice and he was just awful to be around.

To think that I had spent the better part of a decade of my life in an out of control socio-behaviorist personal study of nut jobs was quite honestly one of the stupidest things I had ever done. Why I wasted so much of my time being fascinated by eccentric, bizarre, worthless no talent losers like Riff Mic Stand is beyond me.

Just think, this guy actually sat down and worked on coming up with a stage name and finally came to the conclusion that Riff Mic Stand was THE name for him. Of all the possible combinations of interesting permutations of names that any sane individual could have come up with, *that* was the best he could do.

People would instantly get who he was and understand what Riff Mic Stand was all about. It was catchy, and it had a ring to it. Anyone with half a brain at all certainly could understand that Riff was a musical term and that a Mic Stand only met one thing: a singer with a raspy voice who wanted to publicly be called a Bitch! Riff thought it was cool to be called a Bitch— hmmmmm, I wonder about the subtle undertones of what might have been going on in his twisted subconscious.

Over the next few months working with Riff I learned that he was also a con man, and not just a rasper. His real job was working as a phone sales creep, doing cold calls and harassing enough people where one in, say, 100 finally breaks down and lets him con them into something, just so he'll leave them alone.

Basically, here's how he conned me: he paid me for a bunch of lessons up front and built up my confidence and trust in him. Then, he talked me into recording some demos for him, telling me how he was going to be a big star and how much money I would make later, blah blah blah.

I knew he sucked and wouldn't make a dime, ever, not in a million years, but since he was paying me $30 an hour for studio time, I didn't give a rat's ass what he said.

The thing was, after a few sessions, he started

"forgetting" his checkbook and saying he'd pay me later, etc. I stupidly just went along with it and then out of nowhere we had a tab build up. It kept growing, and then he'd pay me some of it and then it would keep growing. Since, I was an idiot back then and a terrible businessman and a total loser and stoner, I just let it slide more and more.

Somehow, he'd built up a $1,700 tab, and then he pulled an incredible stunt.

One day, he just freaked out on me on the phone and told me that if I didn't give him the tapes we made he was going to drop a dime on me and call the cops on me for selling weed. It was good old fashioned blackmail, at its finest.

I told him he was a motherfucker and that I was going to erase his fucked-up tapes. He got all crazy and tried to use reverse psychology on me and pretended to be all calm and tried to talk me out of it. He was going on and on about his music being genius and how it would be a crime against church and state and all of humanity if I were to act all crazy and erase his incredible music. He kept building up the pressure and escalating the freak show by warning me that he didn't want to have to call the police if I was going to threaten him with erasing his beloved music and that I better keep my head.

He told me that I didn't know who I was dealing with and that he was going to call the fuckin' cops on me and get me busted.

I said if he even dared I would shoot him in the face with my target pistol.

He screamed at me, "don't you threaten me, I'm a member of the J.D.L. and I got my back covered with my boys and I'll fuckin' kill you first!"

The screaming match continued and got worse and then I just hung up on his unworthy, scumbag ass. He called me right back and we fought some more. The threats went back and forth but I didn't want to push him too hard because he was crazy and was ready to fuckin' call the cops and nark on me.

Over and over he threatened me and, after a while, I just gave in.

Riff had me totally figured out. I was in a vulnerable position. He knew it, I knew it, and he knew I knew it. That scumbag freak had me by the balls.

I couldn't afford to stop selling pot and I couldn't afford the thought of having Riff Mic Stand blackmail me and call the cops. It was cheaper for me to give him his fucked-up, shitty-ass tapes and get rid of him than to try and risk going to jail and get butt-raped. Plus, the amount of money it would take to undo the mental damage he caused me would cost me way more in therapy than his stupid $1,700. Remember now, I was and still am, a very sensitive person and not very fond of conflict.

So, Riff Mic Stand got the better of me and after I gave him his horrible tapes, I told him to fuck off and die and to get the fuck out of my life forever. He was such a scumbag and fucked-up human being with no talent — and I mean NO talent, whatsoever. I just let him walk away with God knows how many hours worth of my work, but it was better than risking a bust and ruining my perfect police record and good credit score. Not to mention the embarrassment and humiliation I would feel from my family.

RIFF MIC STAND

I guess if I ever give up music and writing, I can always go into something safe and easy, like stand-up comedy maybe. I can do a whole bit about Riff Mic Stand. I can dress up all in black leather and wear a

121

cheesy, '80's hair band wig, and put on a Groucho Marx nose. It would look funny and BE funny.

The name alone is funny. Riff Mic Stand. What a total scumbag of the earth loser. If I ever see that ratfink again in person, I'll take a crowbar and bash in his skull.

George The Furry Man
(Part One)

I met furry George through a college buddy from Berklee. I've always been fascinated by certain odd types of people and George, an avant-garde artist, certainly qualified as a real eccentric.

He was a singer/songwriter with really catchy songs and he was a pretty decent painter, too. I believe his specialty was acrylics.

George was in a band called The Furry Boas. They weren't very good, but as the chaotic world falls, George stood tall. He basically modeled his vibe after a strung out Lou Reed and a bad version of Bob Dylan.

The main part of the show was watching George try to sing and play his guitar, but the problem was, he only had a four foot guitar cable and he was standing six feet from the mike. So, every time he got to the mike, his guitar would come unplugged, and he'd sing a line or two and then fumble around on the floor trying to pick up the cable, plug it in, strum a few chords, and try to get back to the mike.

The whole thing kept happening over and over. It was a vicious cycle.

On drums, was Percodan Ryan, who played in a band called The Bandwagon. His real name was Dan, but he did so many pills everyone just called him Percodan Ryan.

One time at Berklee, he told me that he took a thousand

hits of acid over one summer. That's a lot of acid for one person. I'm amazed that he survived. I knew a guy in high school who only took acid a couple of times but he had to be taken out of school and sent to some secret mental health facility for a whole year.

On bass, was an ex-con dike named Beaver. We won't get into her story right now, but I think she's in jail.

I don't know how he supported himself, but he probably got money from his family here and there. I know he got a big pile of cash one time and he bought a nice car and some nice clothes and he looked like he was going to be okay, for a while that is. He always ended up back in the same place: the street, or on skid row, or living in a rock 'n' roll rehearsal building.

He told me one time he was living with Percodan Ryan on Hollywood and Western, back in the days when the 24-hour rehearsal place was still there above the pool hall. George and Dan were in a band and lived there for a while. George told me that Percodan was so wasted that he pissed on him and was so fucked up that he couldn't even get up or get out the way. George just stood over him, peeing on him and laughing because he was at least able to stand and wasn't as fucked up as Percodan. The funny thing was, I knew Percodan back in college and he was from a rich family in Bel Air, and it just doesn't matter where you come from. If you're a drug addict, eventually you're going to get pissed on by the world. There are no exceptions to this stark fact.

Furry George came in and out of my life for a few years.

Sometimes, I'd see him a bunch, and then he'd disappear for a while, and then he'd be back in my life all over again. I think he came from a fairly affluent family in Louisiana, but he got in so much trouble with drugs that he was always being kicked out of wherever he was, or living on the street, or staying in a rehearsal studio somewhere. He was definitely a

Hollywood vampire, trolling around on the boulevard late at night on crack.

In fact, George was the only person I ever smoked crack with. I tried it twice. We probably smoked about $50 worth in total. The second time we did it, I saved one big hit and told him that I was stronger than crack and I wanted to give him my last piece because I was so powerful to have that kind of will power.

George was impressed, or at least he said he was, as long as I gave him that last piece. Crack is a nasty and worthless drug that will fuck up your life faster than you can say jackrabbit. But I beat it, and it didn't win and get me, like so many other unfortunate souls.

Cajun Jimmy

I met Cajun Jimmy through Furry George.

Furry told me that he knew the best car mechanic in the world. I needed one because I always owned beat up vans or muscle cars that required a lot of attention. There was always something wrong with my vehicles. Instead of just buying a better car that didn't need to be fixed all the time I figured it was cheaper and more fun to have a private mechanic. Theoretically, Jimmy was going to be my savior. In theory, that is.

When Furry George took me over to Jimmy's house, I noticed he had an engine hanging from an Avocado tree. I thought that was pretty clever. His place was a real mess though, with engine parts all over the place, a bumper in his living room, and greasy tools in piles on the floor.

Jimmy had these two little mangy twin boys, around five or six years old, who were always crying or getting into trouble. He had this white trash wife who didn't have a name. He never introduced her to anyone and she never spoke. Not once. It was a scene right out of *Cops*.

I kinda knew it was a red flag, even during that period of my life when I wasn't too on the ball. I sorta wanted to say something and be nice, but with Jimmy, it was best not to take any chances. He was the king of his castle and I didn't want to piss him off and risk being held hostage indefinitely with him NEVER finishing my car.

Jimmy was a good ole southern boy from Louisiana. He'd tell you that he could fix your car for cheap, and then he'd go to the junkyard and get parts and micky mouse the situation. That means he could do a better job for less by using a sledgehammer or a welding iron to modify parts that didn't quite fit. He'd do things like rig my car just long enough to make it pass the smog test and then put it back to normal so I'd have more horsepower. Jimmy was real good at stuff that was a little sneaky and below the radar. That's how I kind of lived my life and I surrounded myself with people like that.

Jimmy's little sales pitch and philosophy sounded good at first. But the problem with Jimmy was that he would inadvertently break something while he was fixing something else and the problems usually grew and grew and grew. Then, he would get overwhelmed with other customers and put your car on the back burner and it would take weeks, sometimes months, for him to finish.

He was a scary kind of guy, the kind that intimidates you and that you DEFINITELY didn't want to get on his bad side because then you would literally NEVER get your car back.

He wasn't that big but the strength of his forearms and his intensity made it so it didn't matter how big you were because he could make you feel like he would fuck you up in a fight anyway, and it was best to NOT go there with him, at any cost.

I spent years going to this guy and I mean YEARS. At this time in my life I wasn't making wise choices about who I associated with and Jimmy was just par for the course. I probably wasted thousands of hours just waiting for Jimmy to finish telling his old stories about the south to all the other

127

customers who were stuck over at his house with those two mangy kids and his wife, what's her name.

The only way to get Jimmy motivated was to give him pot. So I would go over there on my bike, every day, and bring him some great pot to try and get him to actually do something with my messed up car. At first, he'd start out with good intentions and then something would happen (he would get too stoned) and he'd get caught in some spider web of a tangent and get lost somewhere and the whole day would be a waste.

I'd tell myself that I would NEVER go back to Jimmy once I got my car back, but I kept going anyway, like a broken record, and I must've been literally insane because he would ALWAYS waste my time or break something else on my car so I'd end up paying more than just going to a regular place.

But Jimmy had this southern good old boy charm about him that was infectious and hard to resist. He was a really charismatic guy and should have gone into show business and not monkey business.

I brought my friend Charlie over to Jimmy's one time. Charlie used to drive his dad's beat old Saab, which you could start with a screwdriver.

Charlie and Jimmy were talking about MOPAR cars and parts and crap and Charlie name-dropped a Dodge Charger from 1970. Jimmy got all quiet and serious and looked Charlie in the eye and said, "that's a heavy duty piece of machinery" and Charlie felt all special and in the loop because he knew a teeny-weeny bit about white trash folklore and that the Dodge Charger RT was the one model that had the extra heavy suspension and the fat tires and the big air scoop and all that cool, guy stuff.

I think Charlie now owns four cars: a 1970 Dodge Charger RT, a 69 'Cuda, a 2005 Dodge Hemi Station wagon and a Ford Aspire. The Ford Aspire is the "runner" car he uses mostly because it gets about 60 miles per gallon and never breaks down and he can drive it like a skate board and beat on it and do curb grinders.

Jimmy sold Charlie a shit box old white Cadillac with a 500 engine. I don't know what the 500 meant, maybe horse power or cc's, but it was a ridiculously large engine. I think it was literally the biggest American made engine ever built, or something stupid like that.

It got seven miles per gallon. The day Charlie bought it, he was so impressed and psyched that he was driving literally the worst gas-guzzler ever made. It was quite the pimp mobile. It broke down half a block from Jimmy's house and I don't think it ever ran again. Charlie yelled at me for introducing him to Jimmy, like somehow it was my fault. As if.

Jimmy told me one time that he went to the Hollywood Police auction and bought a beater 60's station wagon for $50 and that he made it last all summer. All he had to do was put gas in it. I was very impressed by how thrifty he was. But I bet he was lying and that the only way that he got it to run was because he knew all the tricks of the trade. Or, maybe he just lucked out for a summer. Then again, maybe driving around in a $50 car wasn't all that cool and more than likely a fire hazard.

One time, I had a big party up in the hills in my bachelor pad, pot dealer penthouse. It was a really big and fun party and lots of Hollywood people were there. Of course Jimmy was invited and he was always a gracious guest. He had all the great stories about car crashes and people's bones being broken and great old stories about back home in Louisiana.

Jimmy was a masterful storyteller; all animated with lots of action. Plus, he was an excellent cook. He was a much better cook than he was a mechanic. Much better. When I would have my big parties I always had a BBQ grill going on and Jimmy was always there, marinating the shrimp and making gumbo with all his secret family recipes. He should've gone into the culinary arts instead of being a gypsy car mechanic.

Everyone was always impressed by Jimmy's cooking. Plus, he had the apron on and had all the attitude of a snotty French Chef from like on one of those TV shows where you just want to punch the guy.

So, my party was going great and I had a band playing on the roof and there were hot chicks everywhere and free beer and everything was just grand.

For a while, that is.

Someone showed up with some LSD and started giving it away for free to random people. Somehow, don't ask me how, Jimmy ended up getting some and he started tripping. Hard. Now, the thing about tripping is that you never really know how someone is going to react because there are too many factors to calculate the outcome. Too many variables. Plus, it was Jimmy, which is too big of a random factor already because you never knew what he was going to do in the first place when he was STRAIGHT.

Nothing really bad happened that night, which was a miracle, considering the massive amounts of illegal drugs and loud music on the roof echoing all through the Hollywood Hills. Eventually, the cops showed up like usual and told us to stop the music and the party slowly dispersed at about 3 a.m.

Everyone had split, but Jimmy was still there, tripping his mind off, running around on my roof deck with his stupid BBQ apron on, howling at the moon. He wanted me to give him a ride home. I was too drunk and stoned so I told him to walk home and just leave me alone. He only lived less than two miles away.

But he didn't want to walk. He wanted a ride. When Jimmy makes up his mind, that's it, he's a one-track kind of guy. He wanted a ride and that was that. So I crashed, locked my bedroom door, and went to bed. Jimmy spent all night in my parking garage downstairs, trying to hotwire my van. He was tripping his mind out and needed something to do to stay busy. Sometimes, with tripping, you just need a fun project to keep your mind going, especially if you're the kind of guy who's a one-track person.

Jimmy stuck a screwdriver in my door lock, broke that, and then ripped all my wiring apart and literally destroyed the electrical components in my already raggedy old beat up van. Nevertheless, he still couldn't hotwire it. I guess Jimmy wasn't as smart as he tried to make everyone think he was. Or maybe the acid was too strong or maybe my van was too whacked to be hotwired.

At 10 a.m., Jimmy called me from the intercom outside.

"Hey Cliffy, can you PLEASE give me a ride home? I just tried to hotwire your van and I can't get it started. Don't worry, I'll fix everything later."

I just rolled my eyes back, sighed and said, "no problem Jimmy, let's get you home to your family. So I gave Cajun Jimmy a ride home and he was still partly tripping out of his mind, but it didn't really matter that much to me because I was so used to being around eccentric, strange, odd, drug addicted and mentally ill people that I actually was partially entertained by the whole thing.

In a bizarre way, it was all mostly funny to me and I thought I had the coolest and most interesting friends. Now that I'm sober, if I were to meet someone like Cajun Jimmy I would offer to take him to an AA meeting and have nothing else to do with him. Every person from my early days of living in Hollywood is either dead, in jail, or in the psych ward. I have permanently left them all behind in the dust.

I actually heard a few years back that Jimmy had gotten sober and was starting to clean up his life. Then I heard that he had died in a motorcycle accident and that his wife and twins moved back to Louisiana. Cajun Jimmy was just another colorful, tragic, lost soul who got caught up in some shit he couldn't get out of — just another casualty of Hollywood.

House Of Weasels
Part 1 — USA

I got a call from an old college friend, who knew about an audition for a rock band. It wasn't to play with the band, but to be a roadie. It paid well and I thought I'd at least check it out. I called and spoke with the tour manager, Wally. He asked me a bunch of questions about my background and my qualifications. I told him that I'd just graduated music school and that I was really smart and that I could figure out just about anything. He said to come on down and check out the band at a rehearsal. I guess they were in a big hurry to find someone.

The band was called House of Weasels and they were an 80's, long hair, rock 'n' roll band. The main guy was an aging keyboard player, named Georgio. I told one of my musician friends that I was auditioning for Georgio's band and he said that Georgio was a rock 'n' roll icon, that he was one of the top three all-time great rock keyboard players. He said it was a toss up between Keith Emerson and Rick Wakeman, with Clay Georgio in third place.

My friend was sort of right, but not exactly. Clay was a really good keyboard player, but I don't know about being third best of all time. That's a pretty tall order. Personally, I would put Jon Lord of Deep Purple way up there, and of course Jan Hammer of the Jeff Beck Group was no slouch, either.

Anyway, down at the rehearsal place, I met the band and Wally, the tour manager, who was about six foot five, bald, well over 240 pounds and basically looked like the strong man from the circus. He was a big guy with a LOUD voice, probably good at yelling at roadies.

James, Clay's scrawny little brother and the head roadie guy, told me what the deal was with the roadie gig. It was basically like any other roadie gig, where you set up the gear, pack it up, and move it from town to town, plus other stupid duties like taking leather pants to the dry cleaners and handing out back stage passes to hot chicks.

But this gig was a little bit more than that. It entailed actually playing background vocals on a keyboard, in real time, with the band, while they lip-synced their parts. You had to have really good timing and know how to play keyboards and know about the technology involved to pull it off. It was actually pretty tricky and a lot harder than it sounds.

Wally gave me the CD and some floppy disks with the background vocal samples and told me to learn all the songs and come back the next day and audition for the band. They only had a couple days to get ready to go on the road, and with those guys, everything was always last minute. Everyone was stressed out because in three days they were going to open up for Joan Jett in Chicago and begin an 80-city world tour. There was a lot of tension in the air and everyone was all high-strung. It was their debut album with a new record label.

Sean Gibbons from LIPS was the president of the label, and he produced the album. Sean was a real character, let-me-tell-you. The first time I met Sean Gibbons was backstage in Texas somewhere at some show, and the first thing he said when he walked into the room of about 20 people, including me, was, "Hey, you guys, I just fucked Jessica Hahn!" Right on, Sean, you go.

I came back the very next day to the band's rehearsal place and auditioned for the gig. It was VERY tricky to have to learn and memorize 12 songs and then have to fly in the background vocals, right on the spot. You only get one chance to get it right, or else it totally messes up and doesn't go with the music and everyone in the band yells at you and you get your ass kicked.

The problem is, sometimes the band plays a little faster

133

or slower and the vocal samples are pretty long, so it isn't hard for them to not sync up, even if you trigger them accurately, so pretty much no matter what you do, it's a little off. But mostly, if you do it right, it sounds amazing. Of course, if the drummer used headphones and played to a click track then the timing would be exact and my job would have been easier. But, since it was a HAIR band, they wouldn't dare mess up their hair just to sound better.

I pulled it off and kicked ass. It was too hard for the other roadies and since no one else could do it, they were stuck with me. I got the gig. I had no idea what I was in for. I just figured it would be fun to go on the road with a fairly big rock 'n' roll band and make a few bucks and bang a few chicks. You know how it is: It's rock 'n' roll, man. I was going to travel the world, see the sights, and have an adventure. Plus, I was gonna get paid! I would've done it for free food and some weed!

I put all my stuff in storage and two days later, I was on the road. We were gone, just like that. Our first gig was on New Year's Eve in Chicago, opening for Joan Jett for the next three weeks. Joan was a really cool chick. Right before she went on stage she'd be wearing a baby-blue, oversized bathrobe and blue fuzzy slippers, like the outfit Carol Burnett used to wear on TV when she was playing some goofy old lady. About two seconds before she went on, Joan would jump out of her bathrobe and walk out on stage in black leather pants and boots and be all rock 'n' roll. It was pretty funny to see her in her Carol Burnett bathrobe outfit minutes before she was transformed into black leather lady.

Joan's bass player was one of my heroes, Kasim Sultan. He was the bass player for Todd Rundgren's Utopia and a really great musician. He also could sing super well and he was an all-around good guy. He had one of those thick New York accents and was a true blue, working musician. Always had a gig.

I got to speak with him a little bit here and there, and I told him that Utopia was my favorite band in the mid-80's, and that it really meant a lot to me, and that I thought he was just a great musician. He was pretty cool about it and kept a low profile. I don't normally just walk up to famous musicians and spill my guts, like a lot of people do. That would be tacky. I'm never tacky. Or, at least, I *try* to never be tacky. And if I ever become tacky accidentally, I want someone to mention it as soon as possible so I can jump out of that character and be back in to my normal, calm, cool, collected self. Or at least *attempt* to be calm, cool and collected. Nobody likes a spazz.

The thing about being on the road with a rock 'n' roll band is that the new guy always gets blamed for everything that goes wrong. I got in trouble, literally, on a daily basis for just about everything you could think of. If something went wrong, everyone would turn to me, and either yell at me, look at me meanly, or throw things, or give me the finger, or somethin'. It was always somethin'.

To make matters worse, I was the most educated, skilled, trained, and talented person out of the whole bunch. I made it clear to everyone that I was, and that just gave them more fuel to go after me with. We'd be at a sound check or something, and someone in the band would call me an asshole for something, and then I'd ask them to spell a symmetrical diminished half-whole scale in C flat and they'd just sneer at me.

One time, Jann, the lead singer, came up to me and said, "Hey, man, where are my leather pants?"

I said, "That's a good question. I don't know. Where *are* your leather pants?"

He yelled at me and said that I was responsible for them because I supposedly took them to the cleaners and I supposedly lost them.

"Sorry, Jann," I said. "That is simply not the case. I didn't lose your leather pants, man. The Creature Sisters probably stole 'em."

The Creature Sisters were these two girls from somewhere like South Bend, Indiana and they were about 18 or 19 and super skinny and small. They weren't that pretty, but they were good-enough looking to want to fuck, and that's what they had to offer.

For a while, that is.

They probably worked in a McDonald's and saved up all their money over a whole summer and loaded up their little crappy car and headed towards the first cool rock show they could find. It didn't matter who the rock band was or what the music was like, as long as they were a rock band that was on tour and on the radio and had some moniker of success; then the girls were gonna find 'em, and try to fuck 'em and hang around backstage as much as possible. They just wanted something to do, so when they finally got kicked out, they could go back to their little, pathetic boring lives and tell everyone about their amazing adventures following a has-been rock 'n' roll band full of phonies that barely broke even, if that.

The Creature Sisters were very determined to accomplish their goals, and boy, did they ever. They fucked the roadies, truck drivers, lighting guys, security, and the t-shirt guys, working their way straight up to the band. Once the band got 'em, they lasted about 24 more hours and then got kicked out of the scene. They were lucky they made it that far.

Every night, it was the same old scene. After the gig, a bunch of slutty, dumb girls would do whatever they had to do to find the band and follow them back to the hotel. There usually was a little line of about four or five girls in front of the lead singer's hotel room. They would wait patiently until he was done and then the girl he would kick out of his room would run out crying and then the next one would run in thinking that she was going to be different, and then ten minutes later, she would slam the door and run out crying, too.

It was pretty much like clockwork — every ten minutes, as long as you were within earshot of the lead singer's hotel room, you could hear the door slam and a girl running and crying.

He was a road dog and he didn't care what you looked like as long as you were skinny and had an okay body, you were good enough for him — for ten minutes, that is. Unless you were super hot, then you'd get treated like a queen and maybe hang on for the whole time the band was in town. That happened once in a while, but mostly it was just trailer-trash – – skinny white girls wearing lots of makeup and all the hairspray stuff and little miniskirts from K-Mart.

The lead singer was the biggest phony of the bunch. He was nothing more than a below-average looking, middle-aged, lame, out-of-work top-40 singer who could only sing good enough to get in this band, for a while.

He was phony on every imaginable level. He had hair extensions, fake, dyed, jet black hair, fake, blue contacts, a nose job, a chin job, a facelift, a neck job, a tummy tuck; you name it. Whatever existed that was fake, he had it.

He didn't even use his real name. His real name probably was Heckter Schmoltz, but he used Jann Hindu to sound all regal and together. He fooled most of the girls most of the time, for about 15 minutes. That's why he'd kick them out after ten minutes, before they realized what a loser he was! He wanted to make sure he kicked them out before they realized how lame he was as a human being and split. He probably had a fake dick too...

Terry was the head road dog. He'd been a roadie for close to 20 years and had seen and done it all. He wasn't too bright, or very good-looking, but he had long hair and looked and acted the part.

And he had balls of steel. For example, he'd walk up to about 30 young girls and blurt out, "Anyone here wanna give me a blow job right now in the back of the tour bus?"

Ninety eight percent of the girls would be grossed out, but there was usually one or two that didn't say anything, or would simply let him take their hand and quickly escort them on to the back of the bus.

Terry had no shame. He got laid more than the rock stars. It was really a matter of technique and the fact that he really didn't care what the girls thought or felt. He was just after numbers, and that's exactly what he got.

I secretly wished I could do what he did. Unfortunately, I had too much of a conscience, but if my sense of morality wasn't there to bother me, I would have been just like him.

Everyone had to wear a backstage I.D., called a laminate. Wally told us that if we ever lost it, our heads would roll.

"No matter what," he said, "do NOT lose your laminate, or else."

All the older, more experienced road dogs told me that if I lost my laminate I could pretty much kiss my job goodbye. I was very frightened about losing it and went to great lengths not to do that.

Inevitably, I spaced for two seconds and accidentally left it in a bathroom. I realized it after about a minute and ran back to get it and it was gone! Someone had stolen my laminate, and now I was fucked! I didn't know who to turn to or what to tell anyone because I was so scared that I was going to ruin my new short-lived career. I was sweating bullets and couldn't believe I was in that terrible predicament where you know you're busted and you just have to wait until you get your ass yelled at in front of everyone.

Right about then, all the roadies came up to me and said, "Where's your laminate, dude?" I was busted. I was like, "You guys, you're never going to believe this, but someone stole it from the bathroom; I just left it there for two seconds, and now it's gone."

They were like, "Man, you're totally fucked and you just got here, too."

They all shook their heads like it was nice knowin' ya and looked pretty grim. I felt horrible and got that feeling you get in your stomach when you know you're busted and in a jam you can't get out of and that feeling is just permeating

138

throughout your entire being.

The feeling lasted for what seemed like an eternity and then the head roadie, James, pulled out my laminate and said, "It's a good thing I found your laminate, man, or your ass would have been grass!" They were all just fucking with me, like usual, but I learned a valuable lesson: don't trust anyone on the road, no matter who they are, especially all my fellow roadies!

The next leg of the tour after Joan Jett was opening up for Cheap Trick. Those guys were rock legends and they all totally kicked ass. I grew up listening to bands like Cheap Trick and even played a few of their songs in high school cover bands. It was a trip to actually meet them and work for their opening act and tour with them.

Those guys partied hard, and I mean HARD. It was amazing to me to find out that they could do blow all night long, drink and fuck young girls, for 25 years in a row, 300 shows a year, and still show up for sound check at 5 p.m., day in and day out. They were like sharks that could swim in their sleep. They were like Zombies that would not die. They were like rock 'n' roll creatures from the black lagoon that could not be killed. They just kept on coming back for more, like sex-starved maniacs on drugs. If there was a nuclear war and everyone died of radiation, Cheap Trick would find a way to survive.

That pretty much sums up the personality type for the majority of rock 'n' roll musicians on the road. If you can think of all the stories you've ever heard about rock 'n' roll musicians on the road, just magnify the story times ten and that's pretty much what it's like.

Drugs, drinking, mayhem, lying, cheating, sexing, criminal behavior, anti-social pathology, paranoia, mental illness, narcissism — you name it — it's all inclusive with rock 'n' roll on the road. It was NEVER about the music. The music was sort of an excuse to be on stage. It was the carrot in front of the horse, the bait for the fish, the spider web for the young girls…

Cheap Trick had this tour manager that was really mean to me. He was always gacked out (that's the rock n roll term for coked out) and always on edge and nervous and angry. He just didn't like me and was rude and mean to me for no reason. Maybe he had a reason, but it looked like he was just an unhappy drug addict and taking it out on me, the new guy.

His mean behavior went on and on for several weeks until one day he came up to me all fake nice and smiling. He said that he was having a problem with one of the keyboard music systems and that no one could figure out how to fix the problem, and he asked me if I would be willing to figure it out for him.

He knew that I was a Berklee graduate and that I was smarter than everyone else on tour and maybe that's why he didn't like me in the first place. His life was never going to go anywhere and all he lived for was drugs, new young girls, and an empty, vacuous lifestyle. We both knew that I had a bright future in front of me and for that, he resented my very existence. Anyway, I always liked a good challenge and even though he was a total dick to me I told him I'd help him out.

The machine they were using played all the string parts for their big hit "The Flame," and they needed it that night in about two hours or else they wouldn't be able to do the song. So, there was a little bit of pressure added to the task. He gave me the device and a pile of technical manuals and I sat down right there and read through it all and figured out the whole problem and made it all work in about 20 minutes. Ever since then, he treated me with a new sense of respect and he quit picking on me. I saved his ass and I guess when you're on the road, if you do something like that, you get a break once in a while.

I was, by far, the smartest guy in the whole bunch. But then again, rock 'n' roll isn't about smarts; it's about being able to survive. It's like being a foot soldier in World War I and slithering through the muddy trenches and not getting killed. It's like being a Russian dude on the Russian front in the middle of winter and almost freezing to death, but somehow surviving and living to tell the tale. It's like that little creature I read about in *National Geographic* that could live for 100 years without air, water, or food in subzero temperatures, and still be alive.

I remember hearing about the infamous Polaroid photo album that Cheap Trick had on their tour bus. The rumor was that they had thousands of photos of them with young, naked girls in all sorts of combinations with legs in the air and drumsticks sticking out, and you name it, they were into it. I never saw the photos, but Terry, the road dog, got invited one night onto their bus and got to see them. When Terry came back to our bus, he told me that the pictures were unbelievable and that it was a true honor to be invited onto their bus and see all their personal, private photos from all the years of debauchery, orgies, and mayhem.

Terry also told me some stories about those guys, because Terry had been around forever and knew everything there was to know about just about every band out on the road. He said that one time, Slash, the guitar player for Guns 'n Roses, and the lead guitar player from Cheap Trick were slap boxing and that Slash was all drunk and got a little carried away and tried to smack the older, smaller guitarist.

What happened then was, Rick Neilson, the lead guitarist for Cheap Trick, the guy who looked like the Bowery Boy with the bicycle hat that's upside down, basically just decided to quit playing with Slash and threw just one punch and Slash hit the deck, and he was out cold. You would think that Slash would be all tough and rugged and all, but that's just not the case. The older, skinnier, more drugged-out and wimpier-looking Rick turned out to be the much quicker and much tougher and resourceful fighter, by far. It just goes to show that you can't always tell a rugged slap box fighter by the cover of the album.

Terry, the old road dog, also taught me some of the

ropes of the road. He taught me the secret origins of "Have you seen Bill?" That was top secret for: "Do you have any coke?"

The way it goes is like this: "Have you seen Bill?" Bill means William. William Holding. Holding means: "Are you holding any drugs?"

I thought that was pretty clever. In AA, the question: "Are you a friend of Bill?" means are you a friend of Bill Wilson, which means, "Are you a sober member of AA?" I guess it just all depends which Bill you're friends with, or looking for; it can make a pretty big difference, though.

I was a pretty cocky guy at times. The leader of the band, Clay, was pretty cocky, too. We clashed heads, periodically. In a rock 'n' roll outfit, a lot of egos are running around, unchecked. Basically, everyone in the band and everyone in the organization, including me, had runaway egos. It was just one big ego fest.

After the initial buzz had worn off about how cool it was to be working for a rock 'n' roll band and being on tour, etc., and opening up for famous bands etc., it got pretty old, pretty fast. The facade of playing it cool to get on the good side of everyone faded away and we all were left with who we really were: a lot of misfits stuck on a tour bus.

The thing about me was, they couldn't fire me because it was too much trouble to train someone quick enough to replace me.

But all the other roadies were replaceable. By the time the 80-city world tour was done, all the roadies were replaced three times over, except for me; they just were stuck with me. They wanted to get rid of me many times, but to train someone else would've been more trouble than to just live with my bad attitude. So, after a while, I wouldn't let them push me around. Except for Wally, he was just physically too darn big to even consider messing with.

Wally told me he used to be the personal security guard for Freddie Mercury from Queen. He told us that he worked for Freddie for three years in the mid-80's when Queen was selling out arenas and it was basically pandemonium at all times. Wally's job was to protect Freddie from crazy fans and to keep him out of trouble as best as humanly possible.

Wally told us that Freddie used to rent out entire floors of hotels with like 100 rooms, just for him and his "friends" to frolic around in after the show. Imagine 1,000 naked gay guys running around from room to room, doing literally EVERYTHING you could imagine, night after night for three years, and having to be Wally (who was straight by the way) who had to sit there and keep Freddie from getting in too much trouble while protecting him from his crazy fans and self-destructive lifestyle. Imagine the Emperor Caligula from way back in Roman times running around in a hotel room on a rock 'n' roll tour...that's what it was like, only without the togas and the grapes. Or maybe not.

Wally had pretty much seen it all and there wasn't anything I could say or do to get over on him. Wally caught me 100% of the time because even if he didn't find any evidence of whatever I was up to, he could tell when I was lying just by looking at me.

I'm a terrible liar.

He had an innate sense of knowing that I was up to mischief, because usually I was and he knew it, and I knew that he knew it. I don't know how I lasted on that tour for nine months, but somehow I finagled my way to stay on that job.

Clay had it in for me, too. He knew that I was a professional musician and a college graduate and that I was going to go somewhere in life. He also knew that I was smart and also a smart ass, just like he was. Clay had a one-liner for everything and even had gags for things that weren't funny.

I would say, "Hey, have you guys seen my bags?" and Clay would say, "What's her name?" Ha ha, very funny, Clay. It was like that every day, at all times. We had a little posturing going on. He was my boss and, technically, the guy who paid me, but to me, he was just an aging, tall, skinny rocker who was pretty smart and reasonably talented, but mostly just a mean spirited dickhead.

One time on the bus, we were sitting around and Clay was saying how great he was at chess. I told him and everyone around that I was an amazing chess player and that I could kick Clay's ass. Clay, of course, did his usual double-take look of amazement that I would have the balls to say shit like that to him, a famous rock star (yeah, right). But I didn't care if he fired me. Good luck replacing ME, dude.

I wasn't totally cocky like that all the time; in fact, I was mostly pretty subordinate and followed the rules and mostly put up with all the rock stars' crap. But every once in a while, I would stand up and say, "Oh yeah? Well, watch me kick YOUR ass at something." This time, it was chess. So, bring it on, brother, it was time to play chess with the leader of the band.

He built himself up pretty good and I actually played it pretty cool, because I knew that I could beat him, and so I pretended that I was just sort of okay. We set up the pieces and had a little audience of a few other band members and roadies and the sound guy.

I moved my pawn to King 4. He moved his pawn to King 4.

I moved my Queen to Bishop 4. He did some stupid irrelevant move.

I moved my Bishop up to aim at the kill square right next to his King.

He did another stupid move, and then I put him in checkmate!

I beat him in four moves!

It's called fool's mate and I hadn't done that since 8th grade. I couldn't believe he fell for such an old trick. He instantly knocked the game on the floor and said that I had cheated. Sorry, dude, I beat you fair and square, and you're just an old retard for falling for the oldest chess trick in the book.

Another time, it was me and Clay at it again, playing cards in the bus and we were playing a really stupid game called Acey Duecy. It's also called High Low, and basically you put down two cards and if the third card is in between the two cards, then you win whatever you bet. If you bet the pot and win, you get the whole pot; if you bet the pot and lose, then the pot grows. This game can last for hours and you just keep on going until, once in a while, the pot grows exponentially and it gets out of control super fast.

It happened one night on the tour bus when about seven of us were playing and a few hundred dollars was in the pot, and then it started to grow out of control. $400 — then $800 — — then $1,600 — then $2,000. People were throwing in paycheck IOU's for $500 here and $500 there.

I had about a grand in the pot and Clay had about a grand in and it was getting late and everyone else had quit except me and Clay. We had a lot of money in the pot and one of us was going to win the whole thing and, you bet your ass, I was going to make sure it was ME!

I'm sure that's what Clay was thinking, too, but here's what happened: it finally came down to my turn and Clay was dealing. He put down a three and t hen a king. Everyone knew I was going to bet the pot because the odds of the next card being between a four and a

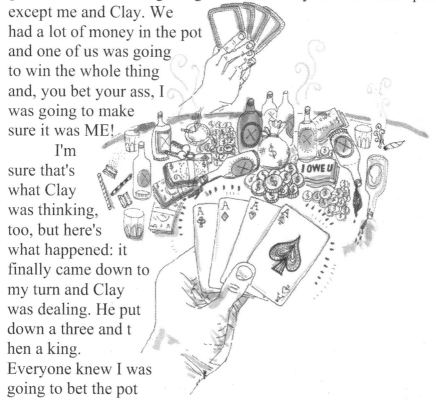

145

queen were very good.

I, of course, bet the whole entire pot, which took a lot of balls I might add, and before Clay dealt me my card, I said, "Keep it fair, dude; take it off the TOP of the deck."

He looked at me with evil eyes like he couldn't believe that a lowly, fresh out of college, young roadie like me would make such a rogue statement, accusing him of potentially cheating. The air was so thick with trepidation that it was electrifying. Clay just glared at me with his beady, little ratfink eyes and slowly peeled off the next card and, YES, I had finally won the whole thing!!

There was a big sigh of relief from the rest of the guys on the bus that World War III had finally ended.

"Not so fast," yelled Clay, as he slammed his hand on the pile of loot. "I'm pulling out a hundred dollar bill for you accusing me that I was going to cheat. If this was the Wild West, man, I would have shot you under the table."

"Whatever, Clay, I don't care. Keep the $100. I won fair and square and YOU are a sore loser."

I only really won about 800 bucks because two-thirds of it was mine, including paycheck IOU's that I had written out, but if I had lost that game it would have been a BIG drag. Of course, me winning like that against the big cheese, old road dog just made matters worse in the long run, but for the moment, I was the cool guy, once again.

Clay, as he always did, would find many ways to get me back, like insulting me in front of hot chicks and ordering me around like I was a peon. But for that moment, I was the MAN, the king dog, the baddest dude on that rock 'n' roll tour bus.

Road Rage

I was driving in my old '67 Mustang on Sunset Boulevard, just a few blocks west of where U.C.L.A. starts. 1967 was the summer of love, and my old beater car had a certain charm about it. But it was mostly just a beater, no matter how you look at it.

Anyway, I was just cruising along, minding my own business, and out of nowhere some preppy guy in a souped up SAAB Turbo starts tailgating me.

I hate tailgaters.

There are different kinds of tailgaters. Some are your typical lame-ass tailgaters who accidentally tailgate you or are just stupid people not paying attention. Others, like this guy, were either on cocaine or crystal meth, or some kind of serious drug, and he was tailgating me within two or three feet, not even remotely close to the three-second rule. This guy was a dangerous menace.

I rolled down my window and used my hand to signal him to chill out and back off. He didn't comply. He just stayed on my tail like a drug-crazed lunatic.

Very calmly, with no malice or negative energy, I tried again. It was a very busy time of day, with wall-to-wall, stop and go traffic, so tailgating someone was not a good idea. Besides, it wasn't going to get anyone anywhere faster. It was just lame. This guy was lame. He was just a crazy, freaked out, yuppie asshole. No more, no less.

I pretty much gave up the idea of being nice to this guy after my second attempt at using the friendly hand signal to slow down and back off. He didn't register. People like that don't register anything, except what they're doing. I guess you could use words like "totally self-absorbed" or "self-centered."

I like to use the words "suffering from a thousand forms of fear," because that's what those people are really doing, although they don't know it. They just think that being an asshole is a good idea and makes sense. They probably think that you have to be an asshole to succeed in today's competitive world. I suppose it works pretty well for most people, but I'm not really very interested in that type of behavior.

So, I made a decision. If he wouldn't back off my tail, I'd just slow down to see how mad I could get him, just for fun. He was fucking with me, so I was gonna fuck with him back.

I slowed down and he started tailing me within inches and freaking out. I was laughing and waving at him. Then, I sped up really fast and he punched it and started chasing me like a mad dog.

Naturally, I slowed down some more so that he was forced to slow down or crash into me. California has some pretty basic laws and if you crash into someone from behind, it's pretty much a no-brainer. It would be his dumb-ass fault and I could sue him and his insurance company for damages and health stuff, etc. He figured out pretty quickly that I was fucking with him and his anger escalated higher and higher.

I was getting real happy. It was fun.

For a while, that is.

All that time, I was just sort of experimenting with human behavior, like I always used to do. Sometimes, you just never know how someone will react. I figured, hey, he's the asshole, he's in the wrong; let's see how he handles some pressure. Let's see how he feels when someone really RESPONDS to his tailgating problem.

So, the fun continues.
Let's do this.

So, now I'm stuck in stop and go traffic, just like he is.

I can't go any faster, and I can't pull over. I'm stuck with a lunatic behind me. This cat-and-mouse game goes on for about five minutes. I slow down, and then I speed up, and then I hit the brakes. Each time I do this, he gets crazier and crazier — and I mean CRAZY.

When I hit the brakes, he almost slams into me, and he hits his brakes and then I can see all kinds of white smoke, and I see his car going sideways and fishtailing.

Then, I speed up some more and he steps on the gas and peels out, chasing me, and then I hit the brakes, and he's skidding all over the road like a total freak show. I'm dealing with a bona fide psycho. Something has to give pretty soon or there might be a little problem; someone might get killed, for real.

The traffic opens up on the other side of the street, so our little freak-show-nut- job-on-steroids puts his hot rod SAAB turbo in first gear and punches it into the opposite side of the street around a corner where no one could tell if a big truck is coming or not. He chooses to take that risk so he can get ahead of me. He literally and figuratively risks his life and the life of countless others just to get ahead of me.

Not only does he get ahead of me — now get this — he does a police maneuver where he pulls in front of me at a diagonal and stops. This totally red-in-the-face, yuppie jarhead dude jumps out of his car in his little lawyer suit and he has that look in his eyes that he's going to try and kill me.

I calmly, and quickly, put my car in reverse, punch it, then slam it in first and PUNCH it again, going around this fuckin' asshole from the Black Lagoon, while giving him the finger and smiling.

For some crazy, lucky reason I'm in a section of the road where there's a right lane open and a quick getaway. I look back, and he's stopped the traffic and is just standing there, waving his arms like a freakin' lunatic punk-ass shithead. I get the hell out of there and take my first right turn into a U.C.L.A. parking lot and hide behind a bush.

This has been fight or flight at its finest.

My life is a LOT more valuable than this guy's. A LOT more valuable. I wasn't going to stick around and see if he had a gun or any golf clubs to attack me with. This was a road-rage freak show violating MY space, not the other way around.

I gave him several friendly warnings to cool it and he ignored them. People like that don't respect friendly warnings. They're Type A predators. Rumsfeld and Cheney types. Anyway, I fucked with him and I fucked with his head. Hard.

Since then, I've learned a valuable lesson: it's NEVER worth the risk to deal with people like that, in any situation, for any reason. There's really no money in it, unless you're a shrink or whatever. I've learned that if something like that ever happens again, to just pull over and let it pass. We're dealing here with an "it," not a human being. People that are "its" don't have any problem murdering strangers, torturing people for fun, raping, molesting, whatever — they're sub-

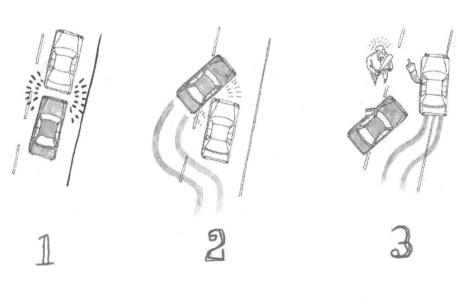

1

2

3

This shows the guy tail-gating me

Then he pulls a crazy stunt and tries to pull me over

150

He jumps out with a baseball bat and I get the hell out of there!!

humans and they're well armed. They tend to be well schooled, too, and quite often have money. They tend to be lawyers or businessmen of some kind. Who knows what they do? I don't give a rat's ass what they do. All I know is, next time I come into contact with one, I'm just gonna let them pass.

"Have a nice day, have a safe trip, bon voyage! Run along now, little boy, I don't want to play with you anymore...ever again!"

House Of Weasels
Part 2 — Europe and Back

The tour was off to Europe for the next three months where we were opening for The Scorpions, Germany's biggest rock 'n' roll band of all time. They were really great, and super regal, like dukes and barons. They'd enter a room with their long hair and gold rings and leather pants and you could just tell they were rock stars. Their wives were all dressed up in furs and diamonds and it looked like they were all just flat-out rich aristocrats.

The band was really nice and polite and total gentlemen, which is very uncharacteristic for rock 'n' roll types. I was very impressed.

It was also my first time in Europe and I couldn't wait to get to Amsterdam, where pot is LEGAL! Of course, when we got there, I jumped out of the tour bus at like 8 a.m., pulled out a little notebook and ran up to the nearest drug dealers I could find, who were about 12 feet away, and found out where everything was and who was in charge and how much all the best drugs cost, etc., etc.

My favorite drug in the whole world was marijuana, and in Amsterdam you could buy it legally in certain public places. It was okay to sell pot and hash in special bars and coffee shops, but you couldn't mix any of it with alcohol; that was available next door. How incredibly civilized and evolved that anyone over 18 years old could go into a hash bar and smoke in public without getting in trouble.

The one I visited every day had all kinds of different types of killer pot from all over the world displayed in little bags in big notebooks. I was in heaven. They had Hawaiian, Kush Bud, Green Indica with purple hairs, Black African bud, and Northern California Humboldt County A Plus Bud.

Legalized pot, how great was that!! This was the crème de la crème of the best pot in the world.

We were in Amsterdam for 11 days and only had one show. We had ten days of R&R with killer hotels *and* we were being paid to just hang out. We got 50 Gilders a day per diem, which came out to about $25 bucks a day to live on (our hotel rooms were already taken care of). It wasn't a lot of money, but it was enough to get by 'cause pot was cheap and food was too and overall, it was a total blast.

I was 24 years old and those were, by far, some of the best days of my life.

When we had to leave, Wally came up to me and said, "Cliff, do NOT bring any pot into Germany through the border.

I saluted like I always did and said, "No problem Wally, you can count on me!"

He said, "Cliff, if you bring drugs into Germany and they find them, then we'll all be cavity-searched, and I don't want to get cavity-searched by Communist Germans in East Berlin. Am I making myself clear?"

"Yes, Wally, I promise I won't bring anything into Germany, and get us all cavity searched. You can count on me sir!"

I saluted again to show him I was serious. Of course, the second he got off my back, I brought a little bit of pot with me, because no one would find out and no one would know and I was too smart to get caught. Once again, I was living dangerously, and, because I was part of a big rock 'n' roll show, I was also risking getting a lot of people into a lot of trouble. But I didn't get caught and everything was fine.

For a while, that is.

We went through Checkpoint Charlie in Berlin, that little "No Man's Land," separating East and West Germany, where they used to have tall guard towers and barbed wire everywhere and Communist German soldiers with machine guns. You walked through this area about 200 feet long where you could get shot and killed for any reason and no one could stop it.

In fact, we heard about a few people who had tried to escape through Checkpoint Charlie a couple weeks before we got there who had been shot to death. It was a little scary and intimidating to think that we were going into a communist part of the world, where life was cheap, and you could get shot if you didn't pay attention or do what you were told.

Well, we walked through "No Man's Land," all well dressed up like rock 'n' rollers, and most of the guys had long hair and wore sunglasses and leather pants and looked all cool, like they always did.

I noticed that way up in one of the guard towers, one of the guards was giving us the finger. He had an M-16 in one hand and his other little hand was just showing out of the window and there it was, his middle finger waving at us.

I instantly thought to myself, "I have to defend our country, I need to defend our honor." I mean, I couldn't just walk through Checkpoint Charlie and not do anything. This asshole was giving us the finger for no reason. I couldn't let him get away with that. He probably was jealous that he was stuck inside his little guard tower world and we could just waltz right through the border with our long hair and leather pants with no restrictions on our

154

lives.

I paused, thought about it for a good five seconds, and very nonchalantly, while we were walking by the tower so no one in my group could see me do it, I gave the guard an upside down finger, which I knew he could see. I just wanted him to know that I saw him do it, and that I wasn't afraid of him and that I was giving it right back to him, in a subtle, little way. Nothing happened after that. He didn't retaliate against my counter offense. No one got shot. No one else saw me do it. Nothing bad happened.

For a while, that is.

We got through customs and no one got cavity-searched. Everything was fine. Wally came up to me and pulled me aside and got in my face and quietly said, "Cliff, do NOT give the finger to Communist German guards ever again!"

Wally NEVER missed a thing. I couldn't believe he'd seen me do that. I'd been so subtle and careful there's no way any normal human being could've seen me do that.

I said, "No problem, Wally," and saluted him, saying, "You can count on me."

He just looked at me like he always did, like he basically wanted to wring my neck and probably would've if he could've gotten away with it.

We made it through Checkpoint Charlie and into East Berlin, where we went sight seeing, and just cruised around. We got to see the Limelight Club, which was in an old, bombed-out church from the 15th century — a very cool joint. I went shopping and bought the coolest black shoes. Germany had the best shoes and clothes, by far, than any other place I'd been to.

For some reason, the Germans made stuff really well, and in general, things were bigger and stronger there. The hotel doors were thick, and made from solid wood and they were taller and wider than normal. The towels were all big and fluffy and better than normal. The clothes were better made and cheaper, and higher quality than what I was used to. They seemed to be tailored to fit my body style more so than anywhere else, except Holland. They had amazing clothes for tall skinny people like me. I'm 6'4" and have long, monkey arms and can never find shirts with long enough sleeves, because normally in the U.S., if the sleeves are long enough the rest of the shirt is for fat, huge people. It's very rare for me to find a friggin' shirt that has long enough sleeves and is tight enough around the chest and waist. I had been all over the U.S. and had shopped in many cities, but nothing compared to Germany and Holland, where just about every store I went to had a huge selection of super cool clothes that fit me surprisingly well.

So, we're all in East Berlin in front of 19,000, drunk and smelly Viking type Germans at the Das Hammer Metal Festival, opening up for Ozzy Osbourne, Motorhead, The Scorpions and tons of other heavy rock bands. The indoor arena smelled really bad and had terrible air circulation. It basically smelled like what I imagine the hull of a Viking war ship must've been like, with the sweaty slaves pulling on the oars while the guy with the whip was being mean to them.

It came time for the show and everything sounded great and I didn't make any mistakes and, once again, it all worked out fine.

After the show, when everything was all packed up and put away, I, of course, snuck off with some chick and smoked a little bit of pot. No big deal, everyone did it, and no one really cared as long as you were cool about it.

I came backstage, looking for some food, like a typical stoner would. Wally was there with a bunch of people and I figured no one could tell that I was stoned and that it's all good. I said something stupid, like I always did, and made a bad joke and no one was laughing, and I just sort of shrugged my shoulders and scrounged around for some dressing room leftovers.

Wally, in a really quiet voice, said, "Cliff, come over

here," and he walked me out into the hallway away from everyone.

"Yeah, Wally, what's up?"

"That was another great show," Wally said.

"Yep, another great show, all right," I agreed.

"Cliff, didn't I tell you not to bring any drugs into Germany?"

"Yes, Wally, you said that, and I promised you that I wouldn't."

"And, didn't I say I would fire you if you risked getting us all cavity searched?"

Yes, Wally, you certainly did say that. What seems to be on your mind?"

"Cliff, you're fired."

Finally, after all those months, I got fired! It almost seemed surreal. Or, maybe the pot was just really good. Or maybe a little bit of both...

Our sound guy, Johner, was standing right there and he hated my guts. He saw the whole thing go down. He had a giant grin on his face a mile wide. He was all smug and just looked at me like a little kid, like "ha ha ha ha ha, you got fired."

I just looked at Johner, right into his little, beady, below average intelligence eyes, and scowled back. Whatever, I didn't care. I was SO over being a lowly, bottom of the totem pole roadie.

I paused for a moment, and then turned to Wally and calmly said, "Well, if you ever change your mind, you can call me anytime and I would be more than happy to go back out on the road with you guys any time, no hard feelings."

He just looked at me like he always did, with a mean grimace, and just walked away shaking his head probably thinking, "Cliff will NEVER learn..."

Whatever man, it was the last show of the European tour; we were going back to the States the next day, and it didn't matter either way. Hey, man, it was rock 'n' roll! I

157

didn't hurt anybody and 19,000 other people were smoking pot, so what's the big deal?

I got back to Los Angeles the next day and since all my stuff was in storage I had to crash at my friend Mike Eddy's little apartment in Hollywood.

Mike Eddy was one of my oldest and most trusted friends in Hollywood. He was my first friend, from the day I arrived. Mike was an eccentric guy who lived in the smallest apartment in the history of indoor dwelling. It was smaller than a single. In fact, it wasn't even an apartment; it was the old building manager's office and was literally just a hole in the wall big enough to barely fit a nest for a small animal.

Mike Eddy was a projectionist for the movie studios and made really good money and could have easily afforded a big house but maybe he just liked living like that. Anyway, he was about 15 years older than me and grew up in Manhattan Beach in the '60's and was cool and I knew he would let me crash on his floor until I got my stuff out of storage and got a new apartment.

I woke up the next day at around noon and noticed that Mike was gone. He was probably at work. I was all hung over and dehydrated and jet-lagged and all groggy from the 18-hour flight back from Germany, via New York. I was extremely thirsty and barely awake, so I looked in his refrigerator for something to drink. I scoped it out and saw an old, unmarked plastic lemonade bottle with some clear liquid in it. I figured it was probably lemonade and grabbed it and took a HUGE chug.

I froze in horror.
I instantly realized what had just happened.
Oh no, I'd been poisoned!

I had just chugged a HUGE gulp of some mystery fluid

that was NOT lemonade.

I didn't know what it was, but I knew it was the wrong thing to drink and that I was totally fucked. I ran to the bathroom and started throwing up white foam for what seemed like hours. I had just been poisoned and I didn't know what it was, but my body was in convulsions and I couldn't stop puking.

I kept puking even when nothing was left. It was, by far, the worst experience of my life when it comes to swallowing the wrong thing and throwing up. I highly recommend to NEVER crash at Mike Eddy's apartment and drink random, clear liquids from unmarked old lemonade plastic bottles. You never know what you might find there. What kind of lunatic stores poison in unmarked lemonade bottles in their refrigerator, right next to the expensive, organic, Berry Smoothies?

After about an hour on my knees, praying to the porcelain throne and throwing up white foam and green and yellow and every other horrible color you can imagine, I gathered up enough strength to call Mike Eddy at work.

"Dude, what the fuck was in that lemonade bottle! I've been poisoned. I'm dying. Help, do something, call the poison people!"

He calmly said, "Oh, that was just pure hydrogen peroxide; that isn't poison. I use that with a diluted solution in my water-pik to clean my gums. It's basically water minus one molecule."

"Quick, do something, I've been poisoned. Help!"

He said he would call the poison control hotline and find out what the deal was.

The poison people said that it wasn't that dangerous, but just to make sure, I should go to the hospital and double check. Mike rushed over and took me to the emergency room in Hollywood at some lame hospital. We got there and filled out all the papers and after about what seemed an eternity we finally got to see a doctor. Actually, it was a nurse, because most emergency rooms start off with a nurse to get the scoop on what the deal is, unless you literally have a bullet wound or got run over by a train; then you get to a see a real doctor right away.

So, I get this big, fat, black nurse who didn't have any sense of humor, at all.

She was like, "What seems to be the problem?"

Mike explained to her that I drank a big gulp of pure hydrogen peroxide that he kept in his refrigerator. I mumbled to her that it was in an unmarked lemonade bottle and that who in their right mind would put hydrogen peroxide in their refrigerator camouflaged like that. She looked at him kinda funny, but you know how emergency room people are, they're all so unimpressed and basically totally desensitized to all human feelings. Otherwise, how could you stand it, day in and day out, with all those messed-up people around you? I guess that's how a lot of people might feel if you really think about it. They have such crappy lives and jobs, and pretty much have to numb out just to get through it all.

Suddenly, for some bizarre reason, and without explaining why, the nurse decided to stick this long plastic tube up my nostril. The problem was, she wasn't very talented or maybe she was just a dumb ass and couldn't get the tube through my sinuses and down my throat. She meanly pulled the tube back out and tried the other nostril.

This one was even worse. She was ramming the thing, and I mean RAMMING it up my nose, trying to get it up through my face and down to my stomach. Of course, she wouldn't tell me what was going on and I was just sitting there in shock, and in total pain and bumming like no other. She couldn't get the tube through that nostril either, so she pulled it out of my face and went back to the first nostril and the madness continued. For all I know, that dumb ass, fat, meanie nurse might've been a sadist.

After about 15 minutes of her cramming this thing up my nose and through my forehead, she finally got it through enough and it started to go all the way down the back of my throat and into my stomach.

At this point, I put my hands up like a time-out signal in football and I yelled at her, "What the hell are you doing to me? Why are you sticking a tube up my nose and down my throat and into my stomach? Don't tell me you're trying to induce me to vomit, because I just finished throwing up for six hours nonstop, and there ain't nothin' left, you dumb ass! If you want to know what I swallowed, here's the shit I drank, you moron!"

Mike Eddy handed her the bottle of hydrogen peroxide. She had that glazed over, stupid look in her eyes, and didn't apologize for traumatizing me. She hadn't even bothered to ask, "By the way, sir, may we analyze what you drank?" Or, "Pardon me, but do you mind if I ask what you accidentally drank?"

That's all she would've had to do. She was just doing a procedure to waste my time and money. We told her up front what the fuck I drank. I should have sued her fat, black, dumb ass and that lousy hospital, too. The trauma of going to the emergency room was worse than being poisoned!

I should've just punched that beady-eyed, ratfink, sadistic, evil nurse in the face and run her over with a steamroller. But I was poisoned, traumatized, and in shock, and not my usual happy-go-lucky self. I had just gotten fired in Germany, been humiliated by all the rock stars who hated me because I was smarter, younger, and better looking, been on an 18 hour flight, jet lagged and all confused and dehydrated, woken up super thirsty and chugged the biggest gulp of pure, 100% hydrogen peroxide — from an un-marked lemonade bottle I might add — right out of my retarded friend Mike Eddy's refrigerator!

I was NOT having a good day.

Finally, a real doctor showed up. He said that I was going to be fine, but that I should stay a couple of days for observation. What he really should have said was that he was positive that I was fine but that he was going to milk my parents anyway for $5,000 with no goddamn legit reason of

161

any kind.

I was in the hospital for three days in my own little room with a TV and three, below average, hospital meals. I could've gone to Vegas, stayed in the best room in town, got a few hookers and I still would've had a couple grand in my pocket for the same amount they raped my parents for.

But you know how it is; the medical system in this country is a crying-shame joke, not to mention the political system and, while we're at it, the military, and let's not forget the energy companies and big business in general. It's all a big mess and everyone knows it. I guess most people just don't give a rat's ass and that's why it'll never change. Or maybe the few people who do care can't really do anything about it because the powers-that-be will just kill 'em because that's how it's done, folks. Might makes right. That's how it's always been and that's how it always will be.

I don't write the rules; I just point 'em out once in a while.

If you want money and power, all you gotta do is rape, pillage, and murder and get in line and take a number, because there are plenty of guys who want to do that, but since the competition is so intense, they have to wait their turn…

After I got out of the hospital a couple of days later, I got a call from Wally and the House of Weasels, asking if I wanted to go on the road some more.

I said sure, man, and I was off and running again.

This time, it was opening up for 38 Special in the south. Now, the south has its ups and downs, like all places, but this one particular place was a dry county. Prohibition still existed and folks were still sore about people having free will to live their lives.

I guess some people will just do whatever they can to try and control other people because they are just plain crazy, and if enough of them get together then, well, they can make a dry county if they want to. That's America in action, folks. If enough people wanna do somethin', then they're just gonna do it, and it doesn't matter if it makes any sense and it doesn't matter if it's legal, or moral or right or wrong. People are just gonna do what they want, because that's what people do.

We were in a dry county somewhere in Florida, opening up for 38 Special.

Wally came up to me and said, "Listen Cliff, we're going to a dry county and that means the people there are extra neurotic about drugs and alcohol. So, please, do NOT mess around with any drugs and alcohol while we're there. Be on your best behavior."

"Don't worry, Wally," as I saluted him once more, "you can count on me."

He just rolled his eyes and walked away, knowing full well there was nothing he could say or do or threaten me with that was gonna keep me from getting in trouble. It was just a matter of time, really.

Everything was cool, and we did a bunch of shows and nothing bad happened.

For a while, that is.

We got a whole new lineup of roadies and one of the guys ended up being a good, long-term friend. His name was Chief because he was tall and had long hair and looked like the Indian chief from that movie *One Flew Over The Cuckoo's Nest*. People still call him Chief to this day.

After one gig in a club, I was just hanging out and some dude comes up to me and says, "Hey, man, do you guys want any coke?"

I'm like, "Sure, man, let's check it out."

So, we snuck back to his apartment around the corner and tried some and it was pretty good, so I got a little bit for the guys, in case they might want some. On the road, there's always someone who wants a little bit of coke but it's not always that easy to find stuff like that, especially in dry counties in the south.

I thought I was doing the guys a favor. I headed back to the club because I didn't want to get in trouble and everything was fine, no big deal. Later that night, I hooked up a couple of the rock stars and they thanked me for being so resourceful and thoughtful. I was just being a good guy and keeping an eye out for them, like I always did.

The next day, we all got invited to a big backyard BBQ party. It was true Southern hospitality and totally fun. Sometimes, life on the road was just a regular ol' good time and this was one of them. We were laughing, and drinking, and eating really yummy food when all of a sudden we hear a big knock on the front door.

"FBI, open the door."

Everyone at the party turned white in the face and we all just froze. Wally and Clay both looked at me automatically, like I somehow had something to do with it.

Turns out the husband of the chick that was throwing the party was an international drug smuggler, and the cops came in and dragged the guy away. They had been doing a sting operation on him for months and, of course, I had nothing to do with any of it. But, as usual, the guys in the band and Wally all looked at me like I was somehow bad luck or something, just because they had to look at someone and, of course, not themselves, because quite frankly they were the ones that invited me, and THEY were the ones with the friend whose husband was an international drug dealer, not me.

So many people are just in denial, in general; they just don't want to cop to the fact that they don't know what time it is in life and they want to blame someone else for their problems. Even though I got some dirty looks from those clowns, I didn't really care, because I didn't do anything, and by that time, I was used to their crap. I just shrugged it off and said, "Could someone please pass the cornbread?"

I Found God In Hollywood

Some people might have a hard time believing that anyone could find God in the middle of Hollywood. But I did. I wasn't raised with a God and I certainly didn't see any evidence in my family that God was an option. We never talked about God and didn't belong to any religion. Not that religion makes you know anything about God. To me, religion has nothing to do with God; it's all just man-made stuff. Some things in religion have nice sentiments, but, overall, I believe it's mostly a con about power and control and the God stuff is just part of the bait.

I just found out from my sister that my parents are atheists. I never knew that. I don't know a lot of things about my parents. I don't even know what kind of ice cream they like best, or who's their favorite band.

Anyway, the topic of religion came up when I was on the phone with my sister and she said Mom and Dad were *positive* that they don't believe in God at all. I always thought that they just didn't know any better. I always thought they were agnostics. Being atheists explains a lot of things to me now. Hey, better late than never.

My belief in God doesn't work like most people. Then again, since I don't physically know most people, there's no way I can substantiate my claim. In fact, there's no way people can prove just about anything that we as a society go along with. Not only that, but unless I was there, I can't really believe what I'm told, or what I read, because, quite frankly, people lie all the time. It's a mean, scary thing to think that just about anything that we're told or read could not be true. But then again, what's the alternative? To believe everything we're told or read? That would be even worse.

The hard part is figuring out the difference between what things people *tell* me are true and what things I *read* that are true. The older I get, the more I can't really tell. I always thought it would be the other way around. Maybe God is playing a trick on me. Or maybe God doesn't exist and I'm playing a trick on me. Or maybe God does exist, and I'm still playing a trick on me. Now, why would I want to play a trick on me in the first place? Maybe somebody played a trick on me when I was little and I forgot how to not play a trick on myself. That could be.

Anyway, let's just say that God is real for now and take a look at the facts.

If you look up at the sky, you'll realize that it keeps going and going, probably forever. I didn't do that. I didn't invent that. I didn't make that up. It's not in a history book and it's not on TV. It's real. Go look and see for yourself. SOMETHING made the sky like that.

If you think about all the stuff you see in life — all the little animals and all the stars and planets — something made all that. I didn't do it. You didn't do it.

So, now we have a situation. It's clear that I am not God, but it isn't clear who is. I don't think God is a person or a thing. It's just a three-letter word that we pitiful humans use to try and describe the indescribable to somehow make sense of the universe and why we are here and what this is all about. Otherwise, it would be less fun; trust me on that one.

Maybe the atheists are having more fun than us. But, my guess is that they're not. But since I don't know all atheists, there really is no way for me to know for sure if they aren't having more fun. Here we are, back to my old theory: unless I know you personally or see it happen, then it's pretty much up for grabs.

I suppose growing up, I always wondered a little bit about God, here and there. But truthfully, I didn't put much energy into the subject until I got to Hollywood. I had to hit bottom in life and truly go down as dark a hole as I could take to eventually come up with a better theory.

It seems that most people in my situation have to go down that dark, scary road, alone and naked, until they either:

A. Go crazy

B. Go to jail forever, or

C. Die

I don't know why it has to be that way, but from my experience, it just seems to be the way God likes to do it. If I were God, I probably would have a friendlier way of doing it. But since humans tend to avoid and reject friendly advice, it probably wouldn't be as effective. So, once again, God has me beat on this one, as usual. But you can't blame me for tryin' once in a while.

I'm not sayin' that I want to *be* God, or outsmart him (or her), I'm just sayin' that it would've been easier on me if I could've just figured out the whole thing without having to go through the valley of darkness — naked, alone, and afraid.

Here's how it happened.

I was in my late twenties, cruising along through life. Just kinda doing my thing, trying to get along with people and have some fun once in a while. I was doing okay, but things weren't really working out as well as I'd hoped they would when I was younger.

When I was about 14 years old, I figured it would be obvious to the world that I was a genius, talented and cute. Well, I have news for you. The world hadn't figured out that I was a genius, talented and cute as much as it should have by then. But at the time, it just really seemed so darn obvious to me. It still seems really obvious to me, at least most of the time. Maybe it's because I know me better than the world does and it's really just a Public Relations thing. Maybe that's what the problem is. I just need a good P.R. lady.

So, skipping to when I'm in my late 20's, I still haven't made millions. I still haven't found my model girlfriend who is my soul mate, best friend and lover. I still haven't been discovered. I still have a crappy car. I still have mean people in my life. I still have crazy friends. I still have that funny feeling that I should generally be doing better in life, but don't know why I can't figure out how.

It happened on July 17th, when I was 29 years old.

I was single. I was driving a '67 Mustang with bad brakes. Still hanging out with my ex-girlfriend, Sandy, once in a while, because she was a cool chick and she liked to smoke pot. I always had a lot of that. Plus, Sandy needed a ride to work and I had a car.

So, I came over to her apartment "one last time." I knew my brakes were bad and I had tried to get them fixed three different times that month but each guy did them wrong and had some big excuse about what the problem actually was. Basically, each guy ripped me off. I think God didn't want my brakes to work so he (or she) could get through to me. We'll get to that later.

Anyway, Sandy and I woke up after our "one last night" and she had to go to work and I had to give her a ride. I told her my brakes were just about gone and that I really should try to get them fixed again and that it would be a gamble if we made it to her job all in one piece. She was a hot stoner chick and she was cool with that scenario. As long as I got her stoned and as long as she let me fuck her, then it really didn't matter if my brakes worked, or not.

Well, this time, on this fateful morning, it DID matter.

So, we got stoned, had sex, and jumped in my beat rig and headed south on Crescent Heights Boulevard in West Hollywood. Sandy lived in a cool neighborhood right below Santa Monica Boulevard. I had to give her a ride to SONY because she worked for some TV production company.

I always thought it was funny how most people got up in the morning and had to go to work. I never had to get up in the morning and go to work. I still don't. For me, I have somehow finagled a way to live my life where I just get up whenever I want to and wander around until something happens and when it does, I'm off and running with a job or some kind of project. Or, I play with my cat for a while, or do some cleaning. I'm kind of like a cat, in a way. I just do whatever I want, and I like to clean. Maybe I'm a cat reincarnated. That's what a lot of the Egyptians thought, so I have read, but then again, who knows if it's really true or not? But it would be cool if it were.

Remember, at this point in my life, I wasn't doing all that great.

Basically, I was 29 years old, white, male, good-looking, talented, super smart, and not going anywhere in life. I had all the advantages you could think of, sort of, But for some weird reason, things just weren't going my way as much as they should have been. But no matter how bad things got, this little flame kept burning in me that wouldn't blow out. It might've gotten really dim, but it never went away, even on windy days.

Maybe that's what still keeps me going when the chips are down. Maybe it's that little candle inside of me that never blows out and makes me want to keep trying and to beat the odds.

Sandy and I got in my car and we headed off. We got about two blocks and I noticed that my brakes were really WORSE than I thought and pretty much weren't working at all. I had gotten to Sandy's house the night before by pumping the brakes over and over, and downshifting until I slowed down enough to either avoid an accident or eventually stop. Sometimes, I had to open the door and drag my foot on the ground to fully stop, kind of like the Flintstones. I went through a lot of sneakers that way.

So, that fateful morning, I was taking Sandy to work and my brakes finally gave out completely, no matter how much I pumped or downshifted.

I turned to Sandy and said, "Hang on, we're gonna crash. My brakes are dead."

She looked at me horrified and braced herself.

BAM!

We crashed into all the nice people who have jobs and were on their way to work that morning at the stoplight right before Melrose

Avenue.

Sandy looked at me like, you dumb shit, now I can't get to work on time. She didn't care about me or my car. She just wanted to get stoned and get a free ride to work.

The accident wasn't a total disaster, but the front-end of my car was all mushed up and the people in front of me had a few thousand dollars' worth of damage.

But my car was still runnin'.

I jumped out and asked if the people I crashed into were okay and they said they were.

I said that I was so sorry, that my brakes had failed, and I would pay for everything and that it was all going to be okay. They weren't very impressed or very happy about the whole thing. People got out of their cars and pulled out their cell phones and started making those calls. You know those calls. To the police, the job, the wife, the yadda-yadda-yadda.

I had to think fast. I was in a situation that could've gotten a lot worse if I wasn't thinking fast. I had a briefcase full of pot. It was full of baggies of eighths and quarter ounces. If the cops came and impounded my car and smelled the pot and then found my bags of pot, then I was busted and that was NOT an option. I couldn't allow that to happen, at any expense. I'm just not the kind of guy who goes to jail. It's not that jail is any worse than how my life was going at the time, but I just wasn't gonna go down like that. Not if I could help it.

I asked the nice people who I crashed into, who weren't in a very good mood at the time, if they could just be cool and let me pay for everything and not involve the police and all that stuff.

They all just looked at me like I was a lunatic and shook their heads like it just wasn't gonna work out that way. They all were calling the cops and they all were gonna do everything they could to get me busted because I crashed into them at a stoplight while they were just minding their own business.

It was my fault and I was going to pay, plain and simple.

I said, "Okay, I'll be right back with you."

Hey man, I would've done the exact same thing if some stoner with a beat muscle car with no brakes crashed into me while I was sitting there minding my own business at a stoplight. As if!

I got back in my car and told Sandy to hold on. She looked at me like I was a crazy person and said, "You aren't gonna just bail, are you?"

I didn't answer her. I put my car in reverse and slowly backed up. I put it in first gear, punched it and did a 180 and got the hell out of there. The people I hit just shook their heads in disbelief while they were writing down my license plate number. They probably felt sorry for me, but who knows?

I didn't feel sorry for myself at all. I had to get the hell out of there because I was not going to get caught with a briefcase full of POT. I'd much rather be a fugitive from the law than just sit there and wait to get busted. At least this way, I had some options. Being handcuffed and in jail has a lot less options, and I wasn't about to wait and see how that might pan out.

I stopped the car by dragging my shoes on the ground until I pulled over to the curb.

I said, "Sandy, get out of the car. You're on your own, girl."

She just looked at me like I was an asshole and jumped out the car.

I was officially a fugitive and in a lot of trouble. The most trouble I'd ever been in so far, in my whole life. I didn't know what to do. I did know that I had to get my car home and off the streets. So I drove in first gear on side streets with adrenalin pumping in my veins, and somehow I made it home without killing anyone or myself.

I told my roommate, Laurie, what had happened. She was in her bathrobe, stoned, and eating some kind of green health drink.

She just shook her head and said, "You know man, that's just how it is in this country. We try and do the right thing, but no matter what we do, we're fucked, man. It's the system, it's the government and it's the bullshit laws in this country that are gonna bring us all down, man. You and I should take this opportunity to get the hell out of L.A. and try something different, like, maybe we could go to Montana and grow pot and live on a commune."

I said, "Laurie, it was my fault, it's not a conspiracy, you stoner. I'm turning myself in to the police tomorrow."

She shrugged her shoulders and said, "Whatever, man. It's your life."

I had to turn myself in.

It was a hit-and-run and about 10 people saw the whole thing and they all had my license plate number and it was only going to take the cops a short while before they were knockin' on my door. I figured I better turn myself in and just get it over with. At least that way, it'll just be a hit-and-run and not a drug-induced accident with a pot dealer.

There were bigger fish to fry than me in this town and the cops were up to their ears busting crack dealers and carjackers and I was way low on the list of people to bust. I really didn't hurt hardly anyone and pot was the least bad of all the drugs; and, quite frankly, pot really isn't all that bad, anyways.

At this point, I had to wave the white flag and admit to myself that, whatever I was doing with my life, my best efforts weren't good enough. I still didn't know anything about God or a higher power, as some people like to describe it, or him or her, or whatever.

I *did* know that I was in a lot of trouble and not looking forward to turning myself in to the police. What was I going to say? Would they throw me in jail? Did I need to get a lawyer? I was fucked, basically. And there was no way out of it. A lot of people in life have imaginary stress and anxiety about what may or may not happen. Not me, I had REAL stress.

If I didn't turn myself in, they'd be after me. Being a part-time pot dealer was already nerve-racking enough without having to worry about the cops showing up randomly while I was selling a bag to someone. That kind of stress was just too crazy for me to handle.

I waited it out until the next day and then went down to the Hollywood Police Department on Wilcox. I was nervous and stood in line to turn myself in. I didn't know what was going to happen. Would they point guns at me and handcuff me and jump me? Who knew what those crazy police would do next.

Finally, it was my turn to talk to the police guy at the front desk. I told him that I was in an accident and that I wanted to turn myself in. He VERY nonchalantly asked me where the accident was and I told him on Crescent Heights and Melrose.

He said, "Oh, you have to go to the Beverly Hills Department. It's out of our jurisdiction."

That was it. He didn't try to bust me or point a gun at me and frisk me or beat me with his billy club. There was no

173

drama. He didn't even care. I was sort of bummed that I wasn't important enough that he didn't show some sort of interest in my case. He was just like, "Whatever, pal. Next."

It took me a while to find the Beverly Hills Police Department. It wasn't that easy turning myself in to the police back in those days. I parked my car in the visitors' area and walked right in the building and stood in line again, waiting for my demise. Would it be jail? Would they shoot me? Would they kick my ass? Would I have to sit in a cell with a crazy black guy who wanted me to be his girlfriend? God only knew what my fate would be.

When it was finally my turn, I told the policeman what had happened and where. I made sure he knew where it was right up front, because I was sort of getting a feel for how to turn myself in for a hit-and-run car accident.

He just kind of looked at me pathetically and asked me why I left the accident.

I had to think of a good one. I couldn't just say, "Well, you see, Officer, I'm a small-time pot dealer on the side while I'm working on my music career, and I had all this pot in my briefcase, and you can imagine what it must have felt like, etc., etc."

I didn't say any of that.

I just said, "Well, see, what happened was, I don't know, I guess I just must have panicked or something. I've never been in an accident before and my brakes went out and I didn't know what to do and I basically just flipped out."

He looked at me like I was wasting his time and he said, "Listen, you need to go to the Pico and Robertson Police Department. We don't handle that area."

Apparently, there are like seven different police departments all over LA and you basically need a Ph.D. for turning yourself in to the police. Who knew it could be so complicated? I had no idea it took this much work to surrender to the police. There should be a drive-through "Turn Yourself In To The Police" window somewhere. That would probably cut down a lot of red tape in the system.

174

So, now I had to *go all the way down* to the THIRD police station. Half my day had been inconvenienced by all this standing in line and driving and getting all the wrong information from those dumb-ass cops. It shouldn't have to be rocket science to turn your self in to the cops.

I was getting kind of annoyed at the whole process and I didn't even really care anymore what they did to me. I just wanted to get on with my life and do my hard time in the state penitentiary. Working on the chain gang, chopping rocks in half with a pick ax, or wearing those stupid orange vests by the highway, cleaning up trash with my feet in shackles next to a big black guy who calls me "baby." That's what I figured I had to look forward to...

I finally find the stupid cop station and just walk in and blurt out, "Where can a guy turn himself in around here?"

The cop at the front desk was like, "Excuse me?"

I said that I was in a car accident the day before and I hit-and-ran and that I wanted to turn myself in.

He said, "Oh, yeah, they already called it in. Here's a form that you have to fill out and someone will give you a call sometime later this month."

Later this month? That was it? No guns. No helicopters on the 7 o'clock news? No cops running and catching air in their undercover, vintage '70s vehicles with a bird named Fred?

Nothin' man, not even a raised eyebrow from no one. I was just another car accident in a long line of stupid car accidents. I had built up this huge scenario of "what ifs," and all I got was a stupid form and "we'll call you later."

At this point, I was so low in my life that I couldn't even get being a fugitive right. I was in a hopeless and desperate place and I had nowhere to turn and no one to talk to about it.

I couldn't talk to any of my friends because they were

all stoners and clueless. I couldn't talk to my parents because they would've just shamed me and called me stupid for being in such a ridiculous situation and then, after all that humiliation, have nothing of value to say or guide me with, so why even go there?

Once again, I was alone, in trouble, naked and afraid.

Well, there was one person — my neighbor, Rich. I knew him from college and we had played in a band before and he was cool. Plus, I knew that he was seeing a shrink and that he was in AA, or something. I didn't even know what AA stood for. So I called Rich and told him that my life was fucked and that I needed help. He told me to go to his shrink, Dennis, that it would be a wise move.

I had gone to my parents a year or so before and told them that my life was falling apart, that I was a pot dealer and didn't know how to stop or get out or how to function in the normal world or how to support myself and integrate myself into society. I just figured all along that the world would just instinctively recognize my genius talent and that it would be EASY to find a great job in the music business.

Guess what?

The music business isn't a real business. It's a bunch of monkeys and crazy people randomly running around without a clue, and most of the time it's just plain old dumb luck to get a gig.

Being a musician and in L.A., where there are literally hundreds of thousands of lame musicians running around getting gigs, just made it harder for me — an actually trained and skilled professional musician — to get noticed and to get through all the quagmire of B.S. Plus, I smoked a lot of pot all day, every day, which might've influenced my ability to be social and motivated and secure enough with myself to actually go and LOOK for a gig.

I remember telling my mother that I was fucked and that I didn't know how to get out of the hole that I admitted I had dug all by myself.

She basically just said, "Yeah, you're right, you *are*

fucked," and that I had dug my own hole and that I needed to get out of that hole, all by myself.

I already knew that, Mom, thanks for the wise words of help, understanding and encouragement.

That was it. There was no one else in my family to ask for help.

I didn't know about AA. I didn't know about nothin', man. I was just in a situation that was so complex and scary and crazy and difficult that it literally would've taken an act of God to get me out of it.

Of course, no one in my family had heard of doing an intervention, which I so desperately needed. That would've been a lot nicer than, "sorry, you're fucked; go and figure it out by yourself, naked, in the dark, on the floor, in a fetal position."

What should've happened was, my family should've taken me out of society and put me in a rehab to detox off of the drugs and TREAT my disease, and gently and kindly HELP me get back on my feet and TEACH me how to be a normal, healthy, productive human being.

But no, I was just pushed back out on to the street, with no tools, street smarts, or weapons to defend myself. Who knows? Maybe it was the best thing for me. Or, maybe it was too harsh of a lesson. Or, maybe my mom didn't know any better and was just like the dog who poops on the living room rug with that far away look in her eyes.

I called Dr. Dennis McCabe the very next day and told him that I needed some help. He was very expensive at $90 an hour, but I had to go SOMEWHERE. I met with him and in the first five minutes he simply said: "Go to AA."

I said, "No problem."

I just needed someone, anyone, to tell me where to go. If a bum on the street told me to go to AA, I would have. I was finished. I was washed up. I was done. I had cashed in my party chips. My way of being in the world wasn't working. I desperately needed help and I needed to have someone tell me a better way. Good thing I didn't ask the Mormon people or Scientology people what to do. If I thought I was fucked then, I can only imagine how much WORSE it could have gotten.

I asked my friend Rich if he would take me to an AA meeting.

He said, "Sure. It'll be fun."

Fun? What was he talkin' about?

Fun? Who goes to AA for fun?

I had no idea what AA was and no idea about nothin'. I was mentally and spiritually bankrupt. I had crossed the line that I said I wouldn't have crossed ten years earlier and was in a spaceship going at the speed of light in the WRONG DIRECTION. I knew it was going to take a long time to get back to earth and get back on solid ground.

Once I started going to AA, everything changed.

One miracle after the next kept happening all around me. It was very strange for me. Everything was strange for me. I was in a ton of trouble with the police and insurance companies with my "wreckage of the past". I didn't know how to function in society or how to hold a job. My life was in shambles, but I still looked pretty cute, even at the lowest point. No matter how bad things got, I always managed to go to the gym and eat pretty well and wear clean clothes.

All the guys in AA were making bets that I wasn't going to last because I would go to meetings with a briefcase full of drugs, but NOT use any of them. They all thought I was crazy and that it was just a matter of time before I broke down and started using.

But I never did.

I remember saying the "Serenity Prayer" while weighing out little baggies of pot, shaking my head, thinking that I really was living in two worlds. I thought that it was going to be a bona fide miracle for God to get me out that situation.

All I could do was go to two or three meetings a day, and then hang out with my new sober friends until the next meeting. I was too scared to do anything else. I was frozen with a thousand forms of fear. Oddly enough, though, I put an ad in the paper looking for a music producer to work in my studio and got a few people to show up for interviews.

One guy ended up being an amazing producer who just needed a studio to work in and he had a ton of clients. The weird thing was, that I overheard him on the phone one day and he said some stuff that sounded like AA slogans and after he got off the phone I asked him if he was sober.

He told me he had 10 years sober! I told him I was trying to stay sober for the first time and that I had a couple weeks clean and sober and that I was a small time pot dealer and that I really needed him to cover me while I went to a ton of meetings to get my shit together. He was totally cool with the whole thing and would work in my studio all day and I would cruise by in between meetings and check in to see how much money we had brought in that day.

It was a true miracle!

Some days, he would make two or three hundred dollars for me, and all I had to do was go to meetings and drop by my studio and he'd do all the work. My brain wasn't able to do any high functioning for a while. I had to focus on sobriety at all costs.

I still had the whole car accident situation to deal with, which basically ended up with me losing my license for a year and having to pay some little fines. The people I crashed into dropped all charges and their insurance companies paid for everything. In fact, I even got my license back in three months for no good reason.

Maybe it was because I quit drinking and doing all drugs. Maybe it's because I went to three meetings a day and shared, and cleaned coffee cups and did all the voluntary service I was asked to do. Maybe it was because I got on my knees every morning and night and prayed for humility and non-judgment and sanity and worked the steps. Maybe it was because I learned that God stood for "Group Of Drunks" and that I was supposed to 'Keep It Simple, Stupid, One Day at a Time" and be of service to the newcomer. Maybe it was because I saved up ten grand and then quit dealing, once and for all.

That was the beginning of how I found God in Hollywood.

PART FOUR

Sobriety

Fuzzy Slipper

My first six months of sobriety was a little slippery. I was still dealing pot and living a double life. I'm grateful not to be doing *that* anymore.

My first shrink, Dennis, was a little too clinical and dry for my tastes, so after about 11 sessions I stopped going. I was in the market for a new shrink and was asking around for referrals from friends and what not. I was going to a regular meeting of AA every week for a while and I considered it my "home group."

One of the women there, who had about five years of sobriety, which I considered an incredible amount of time, told me about her great shrink, Dr. Lisa B. So I got her number and started going.

Lisa was a real pro. She had a Ph.D. in Psychology and had been a professional therapist for 20 years. She had the doctor thing down.

I spilled my guts to this angel of a therapist for four-and-a-half years and this woman knew EVERYTHING about me. I left no stone unturned. She knew every issue, every story, every detail, every thought, every dream; you name it, she knew it. We had a great run, and I believe she helped me immensely through my early recovery.

Lisa was a small woman, about 5' 2" and 110 pounds, with short, bobbed hair and a nice, big smile. She wasn't very curvy, but kind of waifish looking in a way, with small boobs and little hips. Not the typical type of woman I'd ever go for. I always liked the tall, curvy, pretty ones that are more girlie-looking.

Lisa always wore conservative clothes and had a great poker face. She always had a professional demeanor and was a very good therapist. She was an overachiever, recognized in the encyclopedia as one of the smartest young women in America. I think she received some award for scholastic achievement by President Clinton as well. Anyway, she was really together, and smarter than the average bear.

About two-and-a-half years after I started working with Dr. Lisa B, I met a pretty redhead and we moved in together. As usual, we had problems right away and I brought her with me to see Lisa and we tried to work it out together as a team.

My girlfriend was bisexual and a musician and had been in *Playboy*. She was also a part-time stripper. She wanted to bring another woman into our relationship and I was stupid enough to say that it wasn't healthy and that monogamy meant one person.

She also had a lot of highs and lows with her mood because when she was a little girl she had ovarian cancer and had her ovaries removed, which I have learned help regulate a woman's mood, among other things. So, she was WAY moody and we just couldn't find a way to make it work.

Lisa sort of advised me one-on-one that Sara, (the redhead) probably wasn't going to work out and that I should stay strong in my decision to have good boundaries. So, I eventually broke up with Sara because I listened to Lisa B.'s advice and because I was trying to work a good program, complete with boundaries and attempting to be a professional human being.

Everything was moving along nicely and I was staying sober and getting a lot of recovery. I had joined several other 12-step programs and was getting plenty of advanced level recovery and doing the deep, hard, honest work that most AA people haven't gotten to yet.

I won't judge AA, but on many levels it's just the beginning of the journey, and many other programs build from that base and go way deeper into their specialized, detailed, cavernous, bottomless pit.

Recovery, just like anything, goes on to infinity and you can go as deep as you want to. It's a never-ending thing, and if you want to look very closely at any part of your life that's dysfunctional, there's a program for it.

A lot of people say Alanon is like grad school after AA. Some of the other 12 step programs that I went to were like getting a Ph.D., and then some.

The funny thing is, sometimes I still feel like I've barely scratched the surface of my recovery work; there's so much more to do.

Anyway, I was cruising along just fine in my recovery and making some progress in my career and getting a little success here and there.

Every now and then, I'd notice a flyer in Dr. Lisa B.'s waiting room for one of her little shows with her acoustic folk band. She played guitar and sang and appeared around L.A. at little folksy clubs and coffee shops. So, I knew she did music on the side here and there, but we never spoke much about her private life and I never really knew a whole lot about her.

One time, I went to see her play at *Genghis Cohen*, a little supper club in Hollywood that features bands and acoustic singer/songwriter types. Lisa was pretty good and I thought it was kinda cool that my therapist was gigging around town with her little 3-piece girl group. She was sort of like a cross between Joni Mitchell with some Joan Baez. She had a nice persona on stage and had some cute and funny anecdotes as she bantered with the crowd from time to time. She wasn't great, but didn't suck, and it was a fun show.

A short while later, after I'd seen her show, she asked me in a therapy session if I would be willing to do a trade with her. She wanted to make a demo at my studio and trade me her hours for my hours. After she asked me that, I paused and took a good moment to really think about it.

That moment became a turning point for Lisa and me. I didn't know it then, but a lot of things were about to change.

184

I told her, "You know Lisa, I probably wouldn't have been ready for something like this when I was newly sober, but it's been about four years now working with you and I feel like I have come a very long way, and I think I can totally handle producing your demo. Plus, it will be fun."

So, for the next three months, I stopped paying her and we started building up studio time hours.

When the time finally came for Lisa to come over and start her demo she arrived a little late, and had her guitar with her. She looked about the same as she always did, but having her over at my apartment, sitting on my couch in my studio, was a totally different experience. I thought to myself how funny it was and that I had come a long way since first meeting her. I could feel the energy between her and me shifting from her being in absolute control and knowing 100% everything about me to me starting to get to know her as a person outside the controlled environment of a therapeutic office.

Lisa was a bit nervous at first. I told her to breath and stay grounded and that she was safe and not in any danger. I used a lot of techniques that she had taught me about anxiety, etc. I chuckled to myself how funny it was that I was now acting like HER therapist and she was starting to bare her soul to me and expose her flaws and fears. It was a cute moment and it felt healthy and good.

At one point she was saying how she was still uptight and that her neck bothered her, so I told her to stand up and I gave her a nice shoulder rub (like I always do whenever I see a woman in pain in that area). I'm a good hands-on healer type and this was just part of my routine.

She made the usual good sounds a woman makes when she's feeling good and was like, "Ooh, that feels soooooo good." Then we hugged each other nice and slow, like we always had after a therapy session, but this time it lasted longer than ever before and was a lot closer. We were

185

bonding.

Lisa told me right then that she was really lonely. She said that her wife had left her a little while ago and that she was pretty shaken up by the whole thing.

I said "your wife"?

She said that she was bisexual and had loved men in the past as well.

All of a sudden I'm thinking... hmmmm... Lisa is a pretty cool chick and now she's single. I never would have guessed that she was bisexual and had a wife and all this stuff going on in her private life. I always just used to think of her as my doctor and a great therapist I saw once a week in her little office. It never really occurred to me to think about her personal life because I knew NOTHING about it, at the time.

So, after telling me about being lonely and single and liking men, and after massaging her neck and shoulders and back, and after hugging for a long, slow, grinding moment, we ended our session and set up another one for the next week.

Lisa returned, looking a little different. She was wearing a nice, little, short skirt and had a bit of make up on. I had never really seen her in makeup before; she was always kind of Plain Jane-looking and never really wore much of anything on her face. She wasn't bad looking, just sort of average and not very sexy to me because she was small and had little boobs and a little butt and short hair and she wasn't really my type, in general, as far as sexually goes, etc.

But this time, all of a sudden, with her cute little outfit and a bit of makeup, she looked like an attractive woman. She was probably in her early 40's and I was in my early 30's, so it wasn't like too big of an age difference—in the animal kingdom, certainly.

We started working on her song and cruised along for a while and then we took a little break and gave each other some nice massages, and somehow we ended up making out. It was really fun and cute and harmless and it just evolved naturally. She was no longer my therapist, but a single, cute, recording artist whom I had adored and loved for the past four years and who had helped me more than any other human on this planet, and she knew more about me than anyone in my family. She knew more about me than everyone I knew, combined! No joke.

The next week, we started working on her song some more and after we were finished, we started making out and I started grabbing her ass and she started grabbing my ass, and I pretty much just took her by the hand and said, "You're coming with me, little girl, back to my bedroom."

I pulled her pants off and started getting to work right away. We both got naked and I jumped on top of her. All of a sudden, she didn't seem so small because when you are horizontal with someone short it sort of evens up the playing field a little.

Anyway, we started making love and it was okay, not great, but certainly tolerable. She was kind of nervous and had her eyes all closed and she was checking out.

I was like, "Hey, Lisa, it's okay to open your eyes a little and say hello. I'm your friend and let's try connecting a little here as human beings and not just fuck, okay?"

She was really insecure and seemed really awkward and geeky and not a great lover, plus she was all disassociated and checking out every chance she could. But hey, I'm a guy, and I can live with a woman who isn't perfect in bed, plus this woman was a little angel and had practically saved my life. I thought I loved her because she knew me so well and had helped me through so many rough times. Little did I know...

In the middle of sex, I flat out joked, "So, I guess therapy is over now, huh?"

She chuckled back, "Yeah, I guess so."

Lisa and I started going out and at the same time we started playing music together, too. She was really cool about it and asked me if I wanted to play some of my songs. I had never publicly performed any of my songs because I was always too insecure to sing any of them. They were too personal and I had always been insecure about my voice. I have a decent voice, but I don't sing enough and it isn't as strong as it could be, although it's pretty decent-sounding when I get warmed up and don't feel too nervous.

We did a show together at *Genghis Cohen*. Lisa did a few of her songs, and I did a few of mine, and the show went really well. It was my first time singing my own songs at a club and I will be eternally grateful to Lisa for allowing me to work through my fear.

We played around town and did some more little gigs. One time, we played at the Veterans' Hospital for a bunch of old war vets in wheelchairs; another time in a parking lot for a psych ward in Glendale; still another time for runaway teenagers in Hollywood. We were a big sensation for the invalids and runaways!

We had to come up with a name for our band. We both wanted a warm and fuzzy name, but I also realized that I was "slipping" in one of the programs I was in. Slipping means you're slipping back into your addiction or acting out.

When we made up the name "Fuzzy Slipper" we both burst out laughing and thought it was really cute and funny. I called one of my old clients who happened to also be a pretty good cartoonist and asked him to make a band logo for us. He was an eccentric songwriter-artist, old queen and a total character, and he had no problem with the concept of "Fuzzy Slipper."

We told him the basic vibe about who we were, and why we called it that and he came up with a cartoon drawing of two little bunnies sitting in a fuzzy slipper bunny canoe, paddling up stream. It was perfect.

Fuzzy Slipper was born!

I had been going to S.L.A.A. for several years at this point and finally decided to invite Lisa to a meeting because she was DEFINITELY a sex-and-love addict, like me (and 99% of the rest of the world of people in denial). She agreed to go and instantly identified and confessed that she was a true sex-and-love addict.

We both went to meetings together for many months and had a great time. She got commitments as secretary and treasurer, and literature like I had always done, and so we both kept on coming back. Everyone there knew about us, that we were both trying to get help and some clarity on our situation. No one judged us, and it was basically par for the course with everyone else.

There were prostitutes and exhibitionists, voyeurs, and flashers and fantasy addicts and sexual anorexics and everything in between. Believe it or not, it was a very advanced group of people ranging from doctors, lawyers, business owners and creative types. I met some of the coolest and most spiritual people there. As far as I'm concerned, EVERYONE on this planet could qualify for being a sex-and-love addict in one way or another.

But that's another story.

Lisa and I were both going to a lot of meetings and learning a lot about the disease and ourselves and our boundaries, etc. It's quite common for therapists to have sex with their clients; the national average is about ten percent. We also learned that the number of sex-and-love addicts in this country is growing at an epidemic rate, and it's still a mostly kept secret in the media. Once in a while you'll hear about it on the news or on *Oprah* or whatever, but, by and

189

large, it's mostly a secret. That makes sense, considering how our country is based on a puritanical, outdated model that actually creates and promotes the disease by NOT talking about it. The disease loves secrecy and thrives when the lights are off.

We heard that there was a weekend workshop up in Malibu at the Serra Retreat Center, run by Franciscan nuns. I had been there once before by myself and had a terrific time. We spent all weekend going to S.L.A.A. workshops and meetings and did step work and writing and sharing, then had sex all night. It was a total blast.

The whole idea of the retreat was to abstain from sex, and do the spiritual work to heal from our sex and love addiction! My sponsor was there and he knew about the whole thing. But he didn't judge us.

He just smiled and kept saying, "Keep coming back."

He was in school for psychology and was no angel, either. In his day, he told me he used to do poppers and screw up to 30 different men a night in the gay bathhouses of West Hollywood. That's a whole other level that goes beyond the scope of this story. He was a great sponsor, though, really committed to the program and totally of service.

After the weekend retreat was over, I sat Lisa down and told her that I really thought she needed to get 30 days abstinence from sex. I figured that if our relationship was going to grow, she needed to chill out for 30 days so she could get some clarity about us and herself, etc. She agreed to try. At that point, I became her temporary sponsor until she could find one of her own. My goodness, how things had changed since I first met her!

She emailed me the next day and told me that she was going crazy and couldn't make it for one day. She said that one of her clients, Charlie, was hitting on her and that she couldn't resist the temptation. So, she started fucking him. His wife had sent him there so that Lisa would help him with his

190

infidelity and failing marriage. Little did she know that Lisa B. probably wasn't the ideal person to send her sex-addicted husband to.

I told Lisa that she had a disease that wanted her dead and ruined and that she had to do her best to work a good program and find a higher power that could help her stop the madness.

After about 20 days of trying to abstain and slipping, etc., Lisa finally had Charlie move in with her. I told her that I needed to distance myself from her for a while and good luck with her journey. She kept in touch with me via email for about six months, pouring out her soul that she was a sex-and-love addict and couldn't resist fucking all her clients.

She confessed that she had fucked many, many clients. When she was younger, she told me that she had a competition with another female therapist friend of hers to see how many they could get. I'm sure she must have had sex with several hundred men and women that were there to get help from HER.

At about this time, one of the men in one of my home groups approached me after a meeting and asked me if I would be interested in joining his men's therapy group in Beverly Hills because one of the guys there had left and an open slot was available. John P. was his name and he was a very well dressed, highly intelligent and a super cool guy. So I said sure and started going every Wednesday night. It was a terrific group, including a couple of famous actors, a couple of high-powered show biz types and me.

When I first joined, I told my story and they asked me if I had a previous therapist and I told them all about her. They all just looked at me in horror and shook their heads in disbelief and acted like I had been raped or something crazy.

I was like, "What? It wasn't that big of a deal. We were really nice people and just a little mixed up is all."

They kept saying how horrible it was for me to be so taken advantage of and violated and blah-blah-blah...

191

I told them that in most cases it might be like that, but in my case it was different and that it wasn't all that bad and that it was actually a very positive experience — mostly.

They kept saying how in denial I was and that I should report Lisa to the police and Southern California Psychology Board and get a lawyer and sue her and blah-blah-blah...

Finally, after about four months of that, I got tired of hearing all that crap and bailed on the group. When I finally told them I was stopping, the two therapists gave me a 20-page booklet on how "Therapy Should Never Include Sex with a Client" and all the info about how bad it is ethically, and how illegal it is, and how horrible it is to the psyche of the client, etc. I took the booklet with me and carefully put it away in my file cabinet. It sat there for about a year and I just went on with my life.

During that time, I met a girl and moved in with her right away (a common pattern with sex-and-love addicts).

One day, while driving around in Hollywood right by the Hollywood Bowl, I got a cell phone call. It was Lisa. I hadn't heard from her in about six months.

She asked me if I wanted to go to a movie.

I told her that my new girlfriend was in the car with me and that I was off the market.

She said she didn't care.

I asked her if she was still dating Charlie.

She said "Yes."

Then I asked her if he was still living with her and she said "Yes." I asked her if he was right there with her and she said "Yes."

So I asked her, "Why are you calling me now?" and she said that she just had a fight with him and wanted to use me to make him jealous.

Initially I thought that was pretty funny, and that if I were single I probably would have gone along with that, just for fun, but since I had a girlfriend now it wasn't cool.

She sort of understood and we hung up.

Then a bell went off in my head.

That little tramp!

My men's group guys were right!

I should fuckin' report her skinny ass because that's just totally bogus and bizarre.

She wasn't fit to be a shrink and someone should do something about it and that someone should be ME!

When I got home I found the little booklet and read the whole thing. I was going to bust Dr. Lisa B.

The next day, I called my old therapists from the men's group and one of them called me back later that day. I asked him what I needed to do first and he advised me to start with a lawyer and gave me three phone numbers.

I called each one and told them my case. All three told me that if I was a woman and it was a male therapist that they would take the case, but since it was the other way around that they would only make about a tenth as much as the other way. But they all encouraged me to report her anyway, to stop all the craziness from continuing. Not that it's a big deal, but I have noticed MANY double standards in our culture. This country is a mixed-up place, of confused, scared, backward people with a system that not only preys on them, but also has invested billions of dollars in advertising and propaganda to keep people dumb and compliant. We are told we live in a democracy of freedom with checks and balances but the whole thing's fixed folks, I hate to spill the beans and ruin your day. There ain't no money in the banks, the entire business system is based on fraud, the laws aren't real or enforced and there ain't no Easter Bunny, either!

Anyway, I called the Southern California Psychology Board and reported Lisa. They sent a social worker to my apartment and I told her the whole story. She was very calm and patient and wrote the whole thing down in her notebook. I showed her about 80 pages of emails of Lisa confessing to the entire thing and totally busting herself, time and time again. I had photos of us performing and tapes and flyers and a ton of witnesses from the program that saw us acting out all the time, etc. She was SO busted.

After the investigation, the social worker lady contacted Lisa. She didn't try to fight it and confessed to the whole thing. She lost her license and wasn't allowed to practice therapy in the state of California ever again.

A long time ago, Lisa told me that the reason she became a therapist in the first place was because her mother was always threatening to kill herself and her kids, too. As a result, Lisa became an overachiever and a shrink so she could fix her mother. She actually didn't like being a therapist, and she really wanted to pursue music and other creative endeavors. So, in a way, I did her a favor and got her out of a profession that she never really wanted to do in the first place.

I never heard from Lisa again, but the legend of Fuzzy Slipper lives on.

The Water's Coming

I met this woman in AA who was a massage therapist. She sold me her massage table for $100 because she was moving and didn't need it anymore. She was tall like me and it was a pretty big table, so it worked out great.

One time, she took me to meet her friend who was into a lot of spiritual stuff. It seemed like weird shit at the time, but I have since evolved a little and learned a few things. Looking back, I realize I was just clueless at the time and didn't know hardly anything.

This lady had a map on the wall that predicted the future. It was called a Prophecy Map. It showed all the changes in the earth, like where new coastlines were going to be, after all the earthquakes and cataclysmic stuff would happen.

Apparently, there are over 250 prophecies from all over the world saying the exact same thing, from the Hopi Indians to the Mayans and from all the major religions; they all say there's going to be a big problem with the earth around 2012. I looked at the map and thought to myself, how stupid is this map. No one can predict all these changes and with such pinpoint accuracy. It's just a make-believe map.

Or was it...

Years later, I did some more research and found out a few more things about how the planet was changing. I'm not going to flat out say that the map was right or wrong. But I will say that certain knowledge has been presented to me, and I believe that it is a possibility, that there will be major earth changes in our lifetime and just in case these things happen, I want to have that darn map.

I found out where the map was made and bought it online. It took about two weeks to arrive and during that time I told a lot of people about it, how the water was coming and that they better start learning to sail. I told them there was going to be a lot of big earthquakes sometime within the next 10 or 15 years, and that I had a map explaining the whole thing, like that the water was coming and that L.A. would be underwater and that New York would be underwater and that a lot of other places all over the world were going to be underwater and that a lot of people were going to die.

No one really was all that impressed and I guess it didn't really matter all that much to me. It was partly a joke and partly real. I don't mind living in different worlds and I can go back and forth fairly easily. It's not that hard, actually, but I have noticed that not many people want to go there and that it's a fairly unpopular thing to do, so I keep it to myself quite often.

Bill Cosby had a routine on one of his records about Noah and how his neighbor was always asking him what he was building and how Noah said it was an ark and then he'd ask them how long could they tread water?

I always thought that was pretty funny. I sort of incorporated that bit in the routine I told everyone about this map and that the water was coming and how long could YOU tread water. I also used to tell people that they should buy a sailboat and invest in solar-powered stuff, just in case there was a big flood of some kind.

Everyone knows that sooner or later there's going to be big changes in the earth and whether or not it takes a million years or ten thousand or next week, sooner or later it's gonna change.

Everyone also knows that there have been ice ages and dinosaurs and volcanoes and tsunamis and fires and meteors and all kinds of other cataclysmic things over and over throughout the years. It's just geological fact, not some weird idea. Anyway, I was really into this map and couldn't wait for it to get to my house because it was a cool map and I wanted to show it to my friends.

On the day it arrived, I went to work like always. I had a little recording studio on Hollywood Boulevard and Vine in a mangy old 12-story building. My studio was on the 11th floor. I was meeting a new producer/engineer to show him my studio and see if we could get some work, etc.

I met him in the lobby and we took the elevator to the 11th floor and walked towards my studio. As we got to the door, I noticed an odd thing was happening. There was a little bit of water dripping from the ceiling right in front of my studio door. I had never seen a leak like that in my building and figured it was just some stupid pipe or whatever and that it would get fixed soon. I didn't really think too much of it.

But when I opened the door I couldn't believe my eyes. Niagara Falls was pouring through the ceiling onto all of my delicate and fragile music and recording equipment! My entire studio was being totally destroyed by thousands of gallons of water gushing from the ceiling onto my keyboards and computer and mixing board and all of my stuff!

I was horrified and frozen in shock. My prospective client said, "I guess we won't be doing business any time soon," and he turned around and split.

I was in panic mode and frantically started grabbing all my stuff and unplugging everything and dragging it out into the hallway where it was dry.

My whole world was being destroyed by WATER!!!!!!!!

The water came all right, but only in my studio!

It just so happened that the water tower was DIRECTLY above my studio and I was the ONLY one in the entire building of hundreds of other offices and studios with any water damage.

I find that kind of an odd coincidence.

I had been totally obsessed with water coming and telling everyone to watch out and prepare themselves for water destruction coming any second, and then the water came in a completely different way than I was predicting and drenched my whole collection of musical gear. It was a catastrophe.

After I pulled a couple things into the hall I realized that I needed some help and couldn't deal with the entire situation all by myself. Just at that moment, the building janitor maintenance guy showed up with a five-gallon, teeny-weeny pail and walked into my totally drenched studio while hundreds of gallons of water poured through the entire ceiling and he set the little pail under one little stream of dripping water in the middle of the room.

I just looked at that imbecile and said, "Is that all you're gonna do, man? You're just gonna stick a little bucket under less that .000001% of the problem?"

He didn't say a word.

"Call the fire department or the plumbing people," I yelled at him. "Let's run up to the roof and turn off the water mains. Let's do something!!!!!" My whole business and recording studio was being totally destroyed, right before our eyes.

"We have to act swiftly and decisively right NOW to save my life, and that's all you can do?" I asked him, pointing at the miniscule pail.

It was like a sketch comedy from the Carol Burnett show where Tim Conway is the goofy old guy who can barely walk inches at a time and he's the maintenance guy and I'm Harvey Korman who's trying to actually solve a severe emergency.

The old lame maintenance guy told me that he already called the water department and that they were going to come over in 15 minutes to shut off the water leak.

"15 minutes?!!" I asked him. "That's the best our water department people can do?"

What are people going to do when there's 100 billion tons of water pouring into Manhattan? We'll probably hire Tim Conway to put a five-gallon bucket down to solve the problem.

I just couldn't believe the mess that was happening right before my eyes. No one was there to help me, and I had to watch all my efforts of the past five years of building and designing and wiring and learning and assembling all the complicated and detailed recording studio equipment being destroyed right before my very eyes.

Every thing I owned was totally destroyed and soaked, and I mean SOAKED. All my super-sensitive, delicate, DRY, computer gear, and recording gear and keyboards and floppy disks and printers and hard drives were totally drenched!

Thank God the power wasn't turned on or all of my gear would have been zapped instantly. I had NO insurance and I was just basically fucked.

I ran downstairs and told the property managers what was going on and they said that they weren't liable for anything and that I should have had insurance. They showed me my lease and it said explicitly somewhere that they were NOT responsible for any damages in the event of a water leak or fire, or earthquake or all kinds of stuff.

I was a stoner when I'd moved in there five years earlier and didn't even bother reading the lease. I didn't even care or think of things like fires or floods or whatever kinds of things like that. Why should I be negative and a worrywart? Well, I should have had insurance and was just a dumb ass for not having it.

That was the end of my studio on Hollywood and Vine and even though it was a HUGE nightmare and destroyed a lot of my stuff, it was, in a weird way, a GOOD thing. I really was over having a commercial studio in an old, disgusting, dirty, rotten office building and the whole "vibe" thing of being on Hollywood and Vine was totally a joke and didn't matter to me anymore. Been there, done that. I always wanted to have my studio at home where I could wake up and make music and have everything all organized and neat and tidy the way I like things to be.

I took all my main pieces of gear to an electronics repair place and asked if there was anything that could be done. They told me as long as the power wasn't on there was a good chance all the gear could be dried out and cleaned and restored to normal operation.

After all that destruction, it came down to $3,000 to fix most of my stuff.

I told my parents about the disaster and how my entire business had been destroyed by an act of God and once again, they took pity on me and I was rescued.

I think God was playing a pretty mean trick on me that day.

The water had come, just like I said it would, but it didn't quite pan out the way my stupid map said it was going to. Maybe the business of predicting water catastrophes with a Prophecy Map wasn't exactly for me.

George The Furry Man
(Part Two)

When I was about six months sober I was driving down Hollywood Boulevard and I saw Furry George walking along. I pulled up next to him and said, "Hey, man, want a ride?" He jumped in with a big smile. He always had a story and a big smile. He was like a street poet, painter, musician, con man and southern gentleman — all rolled into one — AND he was on crack.

He was the kind of guy you couldn't help but like, but eventually he always ended up pissing everyone off and then he'd disappear for a while and then everyone would miss his fun and games and he'd pop back in for another round of mayhem.

So, I picked him up and asked him where he was going. He said he was going over to Cajun Jimmy's house to stay with him for a while until he got his shit together.

Furry used to drive a cab and he always ended up picking up drug addicts and going on late-night drug runs downtown. He told me that he'd pick up businessmen in nice suits and in about five minutes they'd be off and running to the seedy parts of downtown L.A., copping crack and hookers and all the rest of what the seedy life has to offer. He'd work for a while doing the taxi thing, and then quit or get fired for one reason or another and hit bottom and become a bum and then somehow would weasel his way back into being a partly normal, sane human being for a short while.

I guess this was one of those times when he was trying to weasel his way back in with Jimmy to get back on his feet. Only thing now was, I was sober and wasn't going to just go along with the status quo and let Jimmy get his meat hooks into Furry and get him all drunk and who knows what else.

I thought about it for a nanosecond and then I said, "Guess what, buddy, I'm kidnapping you."

At first, George looked scared, and for a second, he must've thought about jumping out of my moving car. Then, he sat back and laughed and said, "All right, I guess I'm kidnapped."

I think George used to pull tricks down on Santa Monica Boulevard for crack. He'd do nasty things with men, and he told me that he wasn't even gay, that it was just something he had to do to get his drugs.

I knew he wasn't hitting on me, but I also knew that somewhere in the back of his mind he figured he was going to get a free ride for a little while and probably needed the rest. I told him that he had to get sober like me, and that he had to go to AA meetings with me everyday. I told him there were hot chicks there and that he could get free coffee and bum cigarettes and get free donuts sometimes.

He said he would go just for the free stuff and the chance to meet some sober chicks. George wasn't really a good-looking guy, but he did have a sort of charm and semi-charisma that made him pretty darn interesting. Plus, he could write catchy, funny songs. One of them goes like this:

It was amazing, it was a story,
about a boy, his search for glory,
and when he finds it, he's gonna bring it,
home to you, to you, to you ah hoo, to you hoo.

A lot of George's song structures referred to the subject as "it." It was this, it was that, but there never really were any actual subjects. Just a lot of general stories about "it." We used to get into fights about Bob Dylan and I would say how he had a bad voice, and then George would defend him, saying that he was a genius. Furry George was really something.

Anyway, I've now kidnapped Furry George and I'm taking him to AA meetings. He's going along with it all for a short while and gets about 30 days clean and sober. Then he starts wigging out. He starts getting really angry, and all the crap that he drank over and did drugs over starts to surface. It always does, and it isn't easy to deal with or be around. Even though he was having a tough time, George still made a lot of progress and it looked like there was a chance that he might make it. He got a job in a flower store and he started delivering gift baskets and flowers to rich people.

He always got jobs, but they never lasted. Nothing George did ever lasted. He was a good starter, but not a good finisher. I got him a job one time as an extra in a movie and we both showed up bright and early and he got all the free coffee and free breakfast stuff. He started out looking like he was going to be able to hang, but by around 10 a.m. he disappeared and no one knows why he split or where he went. I guess he just couldn't handle being in a crowd, or being sober out in the world. Who knows?

After that, George just started slipping. He told me years later that during this time he would bring hookers back to my apartment when I wasn't there and do crack with them, fuck them, and record them on a cassette machine. He usually made them pay for the crack and either stiffed them on the bill or talked them out of it, or maybe he would pay them once in a while.

Anyway, George called me up one morning, sounding kinda funny. His voice was sort of muffled and he asked me if I could bring over a Batman mask. I asked him why he wanted that, and he said that he got beat up the night before and that his face was so swollen that he couldn't go out in public. He wanted the Batman mask so he could go out and buy cigarettes.

I told him I didn't have a Batman mask and that I wanted to know what had really happened to him. He said his roommate beat him up with a coffee mug. His roommate was a bass player in a band called Green Jello. They had eight bass players, four drummers, six guitar players, and a singer who looked like an accountant. It was a big mess, but in the middle of the show they would have giant, six-foot paper-mache puppets throw lunch meat into the audience. I guess it was more of a performance art piece than a real rock 'n' roll band.

I went over to George's apartment to see how badly he had gotten beat up this time. It had happened before. George isn't a good fighter. He likes to start fights with people who are better fighters than he is.

When I got there, he was so fucked up and destroyed that I couldn't even stomach looking directly at his mangled face. I didn't want to turn to stone, like he was Medusa or something. There was blood all over the place — on the walls, on the coffee table, in every room on the floor, and all over his guitar.

George's roommate was sitting there all calmly, without a scratch. I asked him what had happened, and he said he and George were drinking and that George went into another black out and got all violent and crazy, and started attacking him, and so he defended himself. But George kept on coming, so his roommate had to bash him in the mouth with a coffee mug, and George just kept coming back like a fucked up pit bull.

The whole situation was pretty gruesome. I felt sorry for George, and took him to the local 7-11 store and got him some cigarettes. Then, we went over to Cajun Jimmy's house to show him how fucked up George's face was. Cajun Jimmy was George's mechanic, that is, when George had a car. Jimmy was always interested in hearing about a good fight. If he missed it, he at least wanted to see the carnage afterwards.

So, George walks in and Jimmy's basic response was, who the fuck did this to you? George was noble enough to cop to the fact that it wasn't his roommate's fault but that he had just gone berserk and that now it was over.

Jimmy paused, and considered the situation. He got all serious and concerned. Looking George in what was left of his eye, he told him that whenever he gets into a fight again, he should stop leading with his face.

George probably stayed at my place for a couple months and he stayed sober for a little while and it seemed like he was getting it together. At the time, I was going out with this girl named Wednesday. Her real name was Wednesday Knight. Her father was a famous songwriter from the 50's and thought it would be funny to name his daughter Wednesday. She told me that her dad used to write songs for Elvis and that one time he called her and she picked up the phone and somebody said, "This is E. Is your daddy home?" She thought that was pretty cool. I did too. We were both HUGE Elvis fans.

Wednesday had this little "issue" where at first I thought it was funny, but it got old FAST. We would leave her apartment and then she'd ask me if the stove was on. I'd say I didn't know and we would take a look. No stove on, lets go. Then we'd leave and she'd ask if the cat had water. We'd check and low and behold: the cat had water! Then we'd leave and she'd ask if the stove, the cat and the refrigerator, the microwave, the tv...etc. was on or off or had water. It was a vicious OCD cycle. Not fun, when I was always in a hurry! It took at least a half hour for her to leave her apartment. Poor little, crazy Wednesday.

I was going out with Wednesday for a short while and she had this hot older friend, Cindy, who had about five kids from three different dads. Cindy was a massage therapist and did the "full release" kind of massage where you get the happy ending for an extra 100 bucks.

Somehow, George got to meet Cindy and we all double dated a couple times. At this point, George seemed like he was getting his act together. He was sober a few weeks, had a new girlfriend and worked in a flower store and was going to meetings. The world was his oyster.

Then, I kicked him out of my place because he told me that he was fucking hookers on crack while I was gone and tape recording them. He played me the tape and laughed while I listened, semi-amused by the whole thing.

George didn't care. He just moved in with Cindy the next day. She didn't know what she was doing and George was a pro at this sort of thing. He had to be. They probably lasted a few months.

I just gave up on the guy at this point. I had done the best I could: I'd kidnapped him, made him go to AA meetings, bought him food and let him crash on my couch. George was no random Hollywood schmuck; he was amazing in his own rite, but there was only so much I could do.

I heard through mutual friends that George had put a personals ad in the L.A. Weekly that went sort of like this:

"Genius painter/musician who looks like Lou Reed in search of rich, older woman for fun and adventures."

I think some TV producer lady snatched him up and he lives up in the Hollywood Hills in some mansion.

Furry George was a survivor and always found a way to land on his feet. I always liked George and had a soft spot for him in my heart. I'm glad he's okay now.

Or is he?

The Massage Therapist

I met Marci Winters in the late '80's. I was still dealing pot and she was a referral from my first girlfriend, Val, in Hollywood. Marci was a cool chick. I liked her, and she reminded me of my kindergarten teacher, Miss Blackstone.

Marci was a kindergarten teacher, too, and she was very petite and cute. I always had a crush on her and hoped that somehow down the line I would get my chance. It never happened, though. She always had a boyfriend, or I always had a girlfriend, or even if we were both single for one reason or another, it just never happened. Hey, not everyone hooks up just because one party has a crush on someone. We were pretty good friends though, so that was better than nothing.

Marci used to come over to my recording studio on Hollywood and Vine and buy pot from me and hang out while I worked. She always liked musicians and was always a good hang. I used to give her shoulder massages and she kept telling me how amazing I was at massage. I just figured that any knucklehead could give a good shoulder massage and that you had to be a retard to not know how to give a good shoulder massage. She made it very clear that I was way better than anyone she had ever met at shoulder massages.

After several weeks of coming over to buy pot and get her free shoulder massages, she finally said flat out that she would rather hire me for $70 an hour than use her regular massage therapist. I said I would have no problem accepting $70 an hour to get to massage a naked Marci Winters. I would have done it for free. Hey, it was her idea and who am I to turn down a request like that?

She told me to make business cards saying I was a massage therapist and that she would give them to all her model friends. So, that was the beginning of how I became a massage therapist. I figured, why not get paid to rub naked models' long skinny legs and tired, aching backs?

I knew this girl in AA who was moving and she had a massage table she wanted to sell. I bought it for $100 and then I got some business cards that said, "Hands That Heal." I was ready to rock.

I started massaging Marci Winters once a week and each time I got better at it. It just was sort of an intuitive thing for me, which came naturally. I basically just did what I always did except she was on a table and I did her whole body. I had always been good at massaging women because I had an actual interest in making them feel good. It just seemed obvious and natural to me.

That was it. I was now a massage therapist, along with my usual job of making music and teaching piano, not to mention my secret life as a Jamaican and my other 15 jobs.

I figured, hey, why not massage naked models for $70 an hour? It beats digging graves.

After a short while, I had a few clients and they referred more people to me and I just got better as I went along.

I only worked on women.

Every now and then one of them would get turned on and want to have sex with me. Since I only worked on pretty women, who was I to deny them their God given right?

I'd say, out of the 100 or so clients that I had overall, I only had sex with maybe two or three of them, and I always made sure that the massage was over.

The actual second the massage was over I'd announce that we were officially done and that anything that happened next was between consenting adults. I think that I had a pretty good record and that I showed a lot of restraint.

One of my clients was a pro singer and dancer. She sang back up for Todd Rundgren for 10 years on the road and sang on a lot of his records. She had fake breasts and requested that I massage them. She claimed that fake breasts needed to be massaged often because, if they weren't, they'd get all hard and stiff, like a softball.

It was actually hard work and I would've rather massaged real breasts, but that didn't happen that much. It was mostly women with the fake breasts who actually needed the service of getting them massaged for actual reasons other than for fun. It really was work, and not that fun, believe it or not.

This particular client also was a nudist and liked to walk around naked before and after our massage. I didn't really mind and we never fooled around. It was just like hanging out with a normal person, except she was naked. I never hit on her and she never made a pass at me; it was just about the massage, and she thought I was great. I thought she was a pretty free spirit.

We recorded a song at my studio for one of her voice demos. It was a jazzy song called *Waiting For Godot*. I guess there was some play about a couple of old guys on a park bench that were waiting for some guy named Godot. They went into all kinds of scenarios and details and talked about how great it was going to be when Godot arrived. He never did, but they sure talked up a storm waiting for him.

She had this great older dude who played jazz guitar on her demo and he was amazing. I hired an upright bass player and they already had a killer jazz drummer. I still use that song on one of my producer reels because it came out great.

After a little while, I started putting out ads to get more clients, just to see how far I could take my massage business. One lady called me and wanted to know if I would work on her and her husband. She was rich and lived in the Pacific Palisades and so I just figured I'd give it a shot. I mean, I prefer working on women, but men are pretty much the same thing, so what's the big deal?

They had a gorgeous mansion up in the hills. The woman was very pretty and half-Asian or something, around 30 years old, and the husband was in his 50's, probably, and in fairly good shape, but certainly not in as good a shape as she was.

She was probably a mail order bride.

Anyway, they were in their bathrobes and they were very nice and I set up in their living room and started with her. Everything worked out great and she loved the massage.

Then, I had to do her husband and it was a little weird at first, but only for a second and I just did what I always did and gave him a great massage. He didn't tell me what to do or complain or give me any feedback. I guess I just did a perfect job and there was nothing really wrong. Sometimes people would give me instructions on what they liked and didn't like, but quite often I would just do my thing and they pretty much just loved whatever I did.

My massages were always a little different. I used to improvise quite a bit. It was always so easy and no matter where I started I always figured out a good way to get to everywhere I needed to get to and end in just the right way.

I worked on that couple for several months. But after a while, the wife would start complaining to me about her husband and tell me personal stuff about their relationship. I always listened, and at first, I tried to stay out of it and just do my thing. But I have to admit that I would answer her when she asked for my advice and it didn't take long after that before the husband put an end to the whole thing. I guess he was just a control freak and didn't like her telling me personal things about how lame he was. I told her to bail on him, that she didn't need his money, but a lot of people stay in bad marriages or "arrangements" just because it's too much of a pain to go out and look for a real relationship, or worse — to have to find an actual job. Most people just get complacent.

About six months into my little massage career, I decided to take a few courses on some advanced techniques and maybe get a license. Technically, you aren't supposed to do massage in Los Angeles without a massage therapist's license. Believe it or not, each and every section of L.A. requires a different license. There are about 40 different parts to L.A. and NO ONE ever gets a separate license for each part.

The city of Los Angeles has so many scams and this was just another one of its bureaucratic red tape nonsensical rules that I certainly was not going to get scared into following. Most massage therapists just get the one license for all of L.A. and go wherever they want in its general vicinity.

Anyway, I took a class with a lady who taught a seven-week class in her apartment in Park La Brea. She was pretty cool and taught me a few interesting things. I already was great at massage, but she had some nice methods for where to start and how long to be on each area and how to end. She was very organized that way, and I suppose if you did massage all the time that it would come in handy to have a nice routine. I think it would be cool if most people knew how to do massage, just to be a member of the human race, but that's probably never going to be the case.

I also took a class at the Taoist Institute in Burbank. I forget exactly how I ended up there, but it was a cool place. The class was taught by a kung-fu master, who was also a priest, a meditation teacher and a Chinese healer type — sort of a master craftsman who knew how to do a lot of interesting things.

His name was Carl Totten, and I would say that he was probably one of the coolest guys I ever met. He certainly had his act together and was a very wise, humble and extremely talented and nice person.

I took a class from him called Tui Na, which, according to him, is the oldest form of massage, and he claims that all massage came from Tui Na about 5,000 years ago. Then,

211

again, how could he prove that? For that matter, how can anyone prove just about anything? Let's just say that Tui Na probably is a pretty old massage technique and that Carl Totten could say whatever he wanted to and the odds are that he was probably pretty close. Even if he was making up the whole thing, it didn't really matter, because, quite frankly, who cares where Tui Na came from? It's here now, and that's all I cared about in my stupid class.

Actually, it wasn't all that stupid.

There was also this SUPER hot blonde chick in the class that just happened to end up being my "partner" in class for a few of the experiments on different body parts. It's funny how I end up with the hottest chick in class at a Chinese massage school in the middle of Burbank. Her name was Candy and she was an "L.A.10."

An "L.A.10" is basically like taking all the hot girls from all over the country and then being the hottest one from that group. In fact, an "L.A.8" is like a "Minnesota 10," or an "Indianapolis 10." Then again, there probably are "L.A.10's" in some parts of the country who haven't made it here yet. Don't worry, not ALL "L.A.10's" make it here, but certainly a high percentage of them find their way here.

This town is FULL of "L.A.10's" and I'll tell you, they are HOT. Problem is, most of them have been hit on so many times that they become nasty, mean, self-centered, fear-based, and only interested in one thing: money.

Some want fame and fortune, but it really comes down to flat-out money.

If you break it down, it's like this: a lot of "L.A.10's" are looking for the richest guy and a lot of the richest guys are looking for the hottest "L.A.10." It's a match made in heaven. The problem is, most of the richest guys are older and not very good looking.

So, this "L.A.10" is sort of stuck with a dilemma: should she go for the rich ugly dude or hang out with the poor, cute musician dude?

In this case, my "L.A.10" chose me — for a short

while, that is.

I knew my time was going to be limited with this particular "L.A.10" because it was just a matter of time until she had to go find a dude with a lot of money. I guess they just can't help it. Maybe she was just taking a break from the rich, powerful, mean, ugly guys. Either way, I was grateful that I got to be with a bona fide "L.A.10," even if it was just for a couple months.

Candy was 5' 9" with beautiful, long, blonde hair and a gorgeous figure with a super pretty face and sparkly eyes. She looked like a Goddess that da Vinci would have gotten in a fistfight over in order to get to be able to sculpt her image. She was so pretty and sexy that if she were walking down the street there would be car accidents and men tripping on the sidewalk and literally causing a scene. Her beauty was like out of a movie where there was a wake of trouble following her wherever she went because it couldn't be helped.

She had nice, full C cup fake breasts, but I couldn't really tell until later when I was able to examine her more thoroughly. She kind of dressed in a way that made it difficult to tell unless you were an expert in fake boobs.

Let's just say that she looked real good in a tight sweater.

At first, she was my massage partner in class. She was very serious about her Chinese massage class and she told me that she was a healer. I told her that I was a healer, too. In fact, just looking at her made me feel better. She was a natural!

So we had that in common. Then, she told me that she lived in a multi-dimensional reality and was able to be in three different places at the same time. Without blinking I said that living in a multi-dimensional reality sounded like a lot of fun and that maybe she could teach me how to do that someday. She told me it was easy and went on and on about physics and math and stuff that she read in some way out books. But she sounded pretty convincing and the truth is, it didn't matter to me what she thought because she was so damn good-looking and sexy.

If she told me that she was a squirrel farmer from Kentucky I would have said, "Hey, man, I think squirrel farmers are the coolest." I also would have said that squirrels have always been a passion of mine and that I was amazed that she had taken her interest in squirrels so far. I would have gone on and on about how some squirrels have evolved into flying squirrels and how I have always been interested in the squirrel culture as a whole.

Anyway, Candy also told me that she lived on a spaceship and that she was a Pleiadian. I'd heard about Pleiadians and I'd met people who had said things similar to this, so it was no surprise to me that she thought she was one, too. Hey, I couldn't prove that she wasn't, so, really, it was 50/50 to me.

So, what if she was a Pleiadian? What's wrong with that? I'll tell you one thing, though: if she wasn't super hot and an "L.A.10," I probably would've told her that the odds were she wasn't really a Pleiadian and that whatever crack she was smokin' was getting to her head. I mean, who isn't delusional in some ways? I don't know anyone, and I mean ANYONE who doesn't think something weird about themselves and is thoroughly convinced about a certain thing being right, which just happens to be flat-out wrong.

I know I have been delusional in the past and looking back on that moment I can tell that I was positive at the time, but now I can tell I was TEMPORARILY out of my mind. That's the operative word: TEMPORARILY.

For me, I was lucky. I snapped out of it. Some people never do.

Which reminds me of a funny story.

I had a good friend, let's just say his name is Clarence, who went to an experimental college where there weren't any teachers, classrooms, or grades. But, as he described it, it was more like a project school. You got to do projects. He

214

probably learned more that way, but I'm sure a lot of stoner rich kids just smoked a lot of pot with their projects.

Anyway, my old pal told me that he was dating this chick from another school and she was into harder drugs and what not, and somehow he ended up partying with her and got sort of shanghaied into being her little drug pal. Clarence ended up at her school and was living in her dorm with her, but he was so high all the time he thought he was still at his own school. So, he would go to class and hang out in the quad and go to the cafeteria and everything was going just fine for about three months, while Clarence just cruised through the alternative college life.

One morning, he was hanging out in the cafeteria and had a puzzled look on his face. He turned to someone and asked what state he was in. They looked at him like he was joking and said, New York.

He realized for the first time that he wasn't in Massachusetts any longer and was like, *wait a sec, I've been going to the wrong school for three months but it all sort of looked like the same school and everyone seemed to be going along with the whole gag.*

That must've been a rude awakening for sure. So, Clarence packed up his stuff, broke up with the wacky girlfriend, cleaned up his act a little and got his skinny little white-trash ass back to HIS school, just in the nick of time, too, I might add.

When Clarence was in college he saw a video about an experimental performance art group in San Francisco that made giant diesel-powered vehicles the size of dinosaurs. All of the vehicles were remotely controlled and didn't have any people driving them. Some of them had giant ten-foot circular saws in the front of them with a giant arm swinging a blade around trying to cut the other vehicles. Others had flamethrowers spitting out 50-foot walls of fire that looked like giant dragon dinosaurs. Another one had a 500-pound hammer that was eight feet tall in the front, pounding

215

randomly up and down.

All of the vehicles had a theme and they all were designed to destroy each other. The idea behind this performance art group in San Francisco was to have these giant diesel-powered, dinosaur-like vehicles with flamethrowers and hammers and saws go out in a parking lot somewhere and rumble. I guess whoever was left moving was the winner.

A big crowd would gather and stand around in a big circle with just a little rope keeping them away from the crazy vehicles, watching the chaos unfolding. That's all there was controlling the crowd, a little, skinny rope and nothin' else. No security team, no police, no ambulance, no nothing. Just a little rope.

Imagine a parking lot with about 50 massive dinosaur-sized diesel vehicles with giant saws and jack hammers and wrecking balls and metal and steel arms flailing in the air, all trying to destroy each other in a frenzied, crazy fight with a bunch of skinny, techno geek computer rich kids with their little remote controls running the whole thing.

All the while there's a guy dressed in an Evel Knieval suit, looking sort of like fat Elvis back in his Vegas days; you know, the suit with the big gold belt buckle and the cape and all. This guy is strapped in a rocket-powered go cart and he's got this big 30-foot jump, set up right in front of the giant, rumbling, remote-controlled vehicles, and I guess he's thinkin' about goin' for it right then and there.

Imagine this guy, who looks like the fat Elvis, in his little rocket-sled thingy flying through the air — with no helmet, I might add — right over the top, just barely missing the flailing arms and saws and jack hammers and wrecking balls of steel and metal and fire and hybrid metals and alloys of all kinds, smashing and grinding and cutting and mooshing and spazzing out all over the place with a huge crowd of stoned, alternative lifestyle people standing around in a big circle with nothing but a skinny —and I mean SKINNY— rope keeping all the chaos away from them.

I guess it was a cool video, especially if you like stupid, San Francisco performance art.

Anyway, back to my main story about the Pleiadian, "L.A.10" hottie, who was in my Chinese massage class, who lived in a multi-dimensional reality, and who was a spaceship captain who knew all about double helix D.N.A. molecules and stuff.

She was so ridiculously hot, man.

She used to wear these great little high school girl outfits, like the cheerleader kinds of tight sweaters, with the little pleated short skirts and the high knee socks and stuff.

Man, was she hot.

Who cares if she worked on a spaceship and was good at reciting dribble she read in a science fiction book, like I really care?

I'll tell ya, the POWER I got from going out in public with this chick was unreal. I mean, it was like we would go to the movies and walk down the street and there would be car accidents of guys staring at her crashing into stuff. It was almost like that. I would get these REALLY nasty looks from older rich guys who couldn't get her and I didn't have a dime, man, not a dime. I would even make her pay for the movies and the popcorn and the Raisinettes. I knew we wouldn't last, but I was going to ride that wave as long as I could. Yup, it was worth it, too.

I never really wanted to do massage full-time; it was always just a supplemental income thing, and I preferred working on attractive, healthy, affluent women. But, poor, attractive women were fine, too; I had a soft spot for them and gave them deals just because it was fun working on them and, quite frankly, I would have done it for free anyway, so getting paid ANYTHING was always a nice bonus.

During my time with Candy I had a really cool AA sponsor who was a musician and just a great human being. This was all around the time that the big earthquake happened in Northridge, and my sponsor got a gig working as a building inspector for FEMA.

One night, Candy was telling me that she met with a FEMA guy to inspect her apartment so she could get some cash because of the damages and stuff, and she told me how rude and inappropriate the FEMA guy was to her.

I told her that my sponsor was a FEMA guy and that I'd hook her up with him because he is a super cool guy and not rude or inappropriate.

She asked me what my sponsor looked like and I described him to her. She said he was about that size and that my description was pretty close to this guy.

I said that was totally ridiculous and impossible and that the odds of my sponsor being the same guy as the one who inspected her pad was pretty close to non existent. But still, I was sort of curious to see if it was the same guy, even though the way she described his behavior was nothing like my awesome and amazing sponsor.

My sponsor was a totally stand up guy and NOT some random loser who would hit on a poor, helpless, defenseless "L.A.10" hottie who was in a jam.

We rummaged through her paperwork, searching for the guy's name but we couldn't find it. We went through her closet and looked through boxes and sifted through a bunch of crap until we finally found the work order and stuff.

I couldn't believe it: it was my sponsor after all! How bizarre?

I confronted him the very next day when I saw him at a meeting and I told him about this girl that I had been dating and that he had randomly inspected her apartment.

He said he totally remembered her and that she was crazy and trying to scam the system and that hardly anything was wrong with her place and she got all mad at him for not buying into her scam and that she was a hustler.

But, he did say she was a damn hot chick, and that it was too bad such talent had to go to waste by her being such a crazy chick.

I pretty much had the full story now and understood how two people can have two VERY different understandings of a situation. I had to go with my sponsors story, because you know how the saying goes, "bro's before ho's."

I didn't tell Candy he was my sponsor though, 'cause I'm not stupid. But I knew our time was short and it would be just a matter of time before she had to move on and find a sugar daddy, which, by the way, she very much deserved. It was a fun ride while it lasted and certainly well worth the trouble.

I had another interesting client for a little while. I met her in a 12-step program called Business Owners Debtors Anonymous, and she was a stripper. She had a big house in the Valley and would go to Vegas and strip part of the time and make a big pile of cash to pay for her life back in L.A.

She hired me to massage her big, fake breasts. No joke. It was an actual job. She told me that they needed constant massaging to maintain their shape or else they would get all hard like a bowling ball and she needed them to be worked on. It was actually really hard work and not at all fun like you would think.

After a while, I realized that I was using too much energy in the massage world and getting off track from my music. I also wanted to reserve my energy for just one woman and not spread it out.

Massage was fun while it lasted. I still have my table, and whoever the lucky woman is who ends up with me will be awfully glad she found me. I'm just that good, and I'm not afraid to admit it.

Hey, some people are good at baseball or cooking, or basket weaving, or war. I'm good with my hands. Always have been, always will be.

The Wishbone Incident

The second I saw her; I knew that I wanted her, in THAT way.

Karen was an actress and very talented. She was small, only about five foot two, and cute as a button.

I met her at a party I was having when she showed up with her friend, Karen. Two Karen's. Anyway, Karen the actress was hot, and smart, and bright and fuckin' cool, man. I instantly dug her. It didn't take long either — not to say she was easy — but we both just RAN right into each other as soon as we could. We had a great little three-month fling and it was a BLAST.

One of her favorite sayings was, "I'm all that and a bag of chips."

I thought that was pretty clever.

Karen was from Kansas, and, of course, I had to bite my tongue so I wouldn't say "You're not in Kansas anymore," like she had NEVER heard that one before...

Even though she was short and tiny, she never really seemed all that small. I guess she had a big aura. All I know was, she was amazing in bed and that means a lot to me. I don't know if it was so much that she was amazing, but maybe more like our chemistry was amazing. Trust me, I have FOND memories of her that will last for always.

She told me her dad was always a tough guy and that he would beat me up if I were ever mean to her. I thought that was pretty cool. Then, she told me that her dad was always finding great deals. She said that he was always just in the right place at the right time, as if he was magically standing in the sweet spot of life.

Right after the Twin Towers got hit, her dad was walking by someplace that was selling a bunch of flagpoles dirt-cheap. He bought up all of them because he figured that right after an attack of that magnitude on this country there would be a big need for flagpoles. He was right and made a pile of money. I guess it wasn't so much that he was lucky, but he seemed to know when there was gonna be a need for something.

The morning of 9/11 I was with Karen.

She woke me up and said, "Hey, Cliff, you're not going to believe this, but I think we are being attacked."

I was like, "What do you mean?" and she dragged me out of bed to see what was on TV. I just stood there not really getting the picture, because it looked like one of those dumb action movies like *Die Hard* or something. Only one of the Twin Towers was on fire. About a minute later, we saw a big jet head straight for the other one. It was on live TV and it went right into the Twin Towers. It was unbelievable.

I remember exactly what I said.

"Well, it's about time someone finally did something to this bullshit country of ours! Someone finally had the balls to attack us and maybe it will be a wake-up call for our country, which is being run by huge corporations who pay off our government with bribes and no one is held accountable for anything."

I wasn't happy about the people who got murdered and burned to death or the overall idea of bad things happening to innocent people, but I was simply making a gut reaction statement that in a more politically correct way would sound more like this:

"I guess it takes a tragedy like this to show this country that there are consequences for our actions with other people and that we should treat people better."

I don't think we realize that our actions as a whole are pissing off a lot of people on this planet. I think I read somewhere that the United States is doing a lot of bad things to a lot of people, to other countries, and to this planet and our government is lying flat out to us about what's really going on. I'm not really anti-U.S. but I am anti-bullshit and having

221

bullshit artists constantly lying to me.

I love this country, but I don't love George Bush and his trigger happy, criminal administration. I believe that he flat out cheated to win the election and lied through his teeth about Iraq and he's just a low-class bum who's stealing oil and murdering people all day long. He's just one below-average-rich-kid-con-man-spineless-flunky, who unfortunately happened to be the most powerful leader in the world, which isn't saying much, but it is pretty embarrassing to be an American these days.

Anyway, Karen was really awesome and I loved our little three-month fling. We got along great. Most of the time, that is. A couple of goofy little situations ultimately destroyed us.

I took her back east to meet my family, because my sister was getting married and I thought it would be fun to bring Karen. I paid to fly her out and she was just wonderful to have around.

But not everything went smoothly.

The airline made a big mistake and we had to sit at the airport for seven hours, waiting for some dumb plane to get its shit together. When we finally got on the plane we had to sit apart from each other.

Karen just broke down and started crying; she couldn't take it anymore. She was SUCH a good actress. Man, was I impressed. I don't think this time she was acting, but one never really knows when you're with an amazing actress; they are so good at working their emotions.

Anyway, I told her that I would stick by her and if she wanted to get off the plane and wait for another one so we could be together than I would do whatever it took to be by her side.

I was chivalrous all right. One of the guys on the plane was so impressed by my valiant behavior that he offered up his seat so that we could both sit next to each other.

222

Karen was so cute when she cried. Man, you should have seen her — that cute little face and her cute little butt. Anyway, the flight was from hell, but we finally made it to the east coast to hang out with my family.

My sister was getting married and it was gonna be a Jewish wedding, so I had to wear the funny little hat and carry some tent around in front of everyone. It was an awesome wedding and I hadn't seen some of the people there for 20 years. Much of my family had been scattered because of divorces and what not.

Anyway, I'm in the music business and my sister is marrying a guy who has a cousin who is a BIG SHOT in the music business. My sister is no dope, so she makes sure that me and my new cousin-in-law sit at the same table. She tells me all about him, etc., and I try to keep it together and not make it look like a setup. I figure I'll wait until the right moment and then tell him about all my amazing record projects, etc.

Karen, by the way, used to go out with a big dog in the record business, who will remain nameless to protect the innocent, but let's just call him John K. He's the guy who used to wear the big white suits who was always ripping off John Lennon's image with the long beard, etc. Anyway, he was a big dog and Karen went out with him for three years. After they broke up, he bought her a brand new Mercedes sedan! That was nice of him. Well, I was broke and didn't give her anything except just plain ole me and that old big dog might still be missing her. If I'd had money though, I would've bought her all kinds of things. That woman was WORTH IT; let me tell you!!!!!!!!!

So, after about three hours of the wedding and hanging out at the table, I finally got my chance with my new cousin-in-law, the big dog record biz guy. I heard him say that he just read the *Celestine Prophecy* and I jumped in and said, "Man, that was the best book. I read that thing three times!" Which

223

was true, by the way. He was impressed. We had a really intense talk about synchronicity and all the coincidences of life and how it's really more than just a coincidence about many things. I told him that I was so into the book that I started underlining lines in the book and making notes and writing down bits and pieces to further educate myself about the material, etc.

He was impressed. I wasn't trying to impress him, but I was just telling him what I did. We had a big conversation and then we segued into other books and just rambled on for a little while longer. At the end of the night, he gave me his business card and said that he knew I was a music producer and that if I wanted to send him some music, he'd take a listen. He said he couldn't promise anything, but that he would give me a shot.

All I wanted was a shot. I never wanted any handouts; I just wanted a fair shot. That's all I really want in life in general is a fair shot. I should call myself "Fair Shot Brodsky: That's All I Really Want In Life."

Karen got along great with everyone at the wedding and totally impressed them all by how cool she was. My new cousin-in-law still asks about Karen and still comments on how cool she was.

She was a cool fuckin' chick, man. She had a way about her that made people feel easy to be themselves; maybe it was because she was small and not big enough to kick anyone's ass, which could have made people not feel threatened by her. Or, maybe it was because she genuinely had a gift about her that made people feel comfortable. Or maybe it was because she was just a great actress and knew how to work a room. I'll never know for sure. But one thing was for certain: she was a cool fuckin' chick!

The wedding went great and Karen and I had a blast and visited with my whole family and everyone loved her. Things were looking great.

I should mention one thing, however. She was about eight years older than I was, even though that doesn't really matter. I just thought that people should know at some point in the story.

Let me tell you, man. This chick had some EXPERIENCE. She had been married before and lived in New York City and hung out with Madonna before she made it.

Karen told me a story about Madonna. She said that her husband used to be in a band and he rehearsed in the same building that Madonna rehearsed in before she became known. Madonna was just basically a club chick who could dance and BARELY sing. That's still true today.

Anyway, Karen told me that a pimp came to the building looking to recruit hookers. Madonna, without flinching, of course, ran after the guy and begged him so that she could get a job, doing what women do. The story goes that she got turned down by the pimp because she wasn't hot enough, or sexy enough, or nasty enough, or for whatever reason, like maybe because she was TOO nasty and didn't shave under her armpits (which I think was the actual reason why she got turned down to be a prostitute).

I think that's funny in a way, that Madonna couldn't even get a gig as a prostitute, but ended up being a HUGE MOGUL in the music industry. I guess that might say a little about what the music industry is like. Feel free to take liberties guessing.

And now, it's time to tell about the wishbone incident.

It was around Thanksgiving and there was a wishbone sitting on a table in my apartment.

Karen said, "Hey, let's play the wishbone game."

I said, "OK, let's play!"

She picked up the wishbone and we were gonna pull it apart when I said, "Hey, wait a second."

She was like, "What?" She was holding the wishbone

about halfway up and I was holding it at the tip like you're supposed to. I pointed out to her that she was supposed to hold it at the end like I was.

She just looked at me horrified, like I was the grim reaper, and angrily laughed at me, like I was an idiot, and said, "You hold it the way you want to and I'll hold it the way I want to, and let's fuckin' play the stupid game!"

I was like, "Well, here's the thing. If you hold it halfway up, you're going to win and it's not fair. Everyone knows you're supposed to hold it at the bottom so it will be a fair fight."

She said I was crazy and that she had never heard that before and that I was being a total jerk. She was getting all irate and angry and red in the face.

I said, "Time out. Let's hold off on the wishbone game and see if we can talk about what's really going on."

She just looked at me like I was Satan and couldn't believe that I was such a total loser and jerk that I would be so controlling as to make her play the wishbone game a certain way. She started yelling at me and dancing around the kitchen with the wishbone threatening to break it in half herself so no one could play the game.

I was like, "So that's how you wanna play this? If we can't do it your way, you're going to ruin the game so no one else can play? Is that how you were as a little kid in school? If people couldn't play the way you wanted, you were going to wreck the game? If you had a kickball and no one would let you play, would you poke a hole in the ball so it wouldn't

226

work? If all the kids were making a house of cards and wouldn't let you play, would you just knock it over and ruin all their fun?"

You can see where this was going...

I said, "Listen, woman, this isn't about the wishbone game. This is about something else, and I want to sit down with you and work it out because I don't want us to have a miscommunication about something and have a fight over literally nothing just because there was a misunderstanding."

She said, "Okay, let's sit down and see what you have to say."

She was a very intelligent, and spiritual person, and I think she really had a great heart and she wanted things to go well. I don't think she was aware that she was having a spontaneous age regression and was clueless that EVERYONE KNOWS YOU'RE SUPPOSED TO HOLD THE WISHBONE BY THE TIP, NOT HALFWAY UP, MAN!

But, that could just be one of my issues and I'm willing to take a look at it.

We sat down on my couch and I said that I 'd been reading a lot of John Bradshaw books and he said that a lot of families have different rituals and sometimes during Christmas, for example, some people open all the presents at the same time and there's anarchy and that's just how they do it. Other people like to open the presents one at a time and talk about them and write down in a little book who gave them the present and what it was so they can keep track of all their little gifts and be organized about how they were going to send their thank-you letters. Some people saved the boxes and the ribbons, and some people threw everything away. It doesn't make one person or family better or worse, but simply DIFFERENT.

I was trying to say in a nice way that people do things differently and that it wasn't about the wishbone game per se, but that we should be able to make compromises and figure

227

out a happy medium.

The problem with the wishbone incident was that I was right and she was wrong, and why should I play along with her cockamamie idea that there isn't a standardized way to hold the wishbone, when it's a plain fact that there is only ONE way to hold the wishbone and it's common knowledge.

Karen told me that I was just making that up and where she comes from, since as far back as she can remember, everyone holds the wishbone from the middle. She couldn't understand why I wouldn't hold the wishbone from the middle, like her. It would be an even match that way.

True, I said, it would have come out the same, but I knew for a fact that you're supposed to hold it from the bottom and that it would be better and that she should do it my way because it was better.

I think that maybe I should have just held it in the middle because of one simple fact: Karen had such a great little body that I so adored, and I mean ADORED, that it was a pretty small price to pay to keep that show runnin'.

Man, I should have just gone along with her little game. I was such an idiot. Who cares if I was right? It pissed her off and that was the second-to-last straw for her. She was the kind of chick that if you crossed her, man, that was it. She was a tough little cookie. But, GOD, did she have the most perfect little body you could ever believe. I still think about her in *that* way sometimes.

She also was super pretty. It wasn't just about her perfect little ass, but it was a pretty important factor in my brain and I'm just being honest here because let's face it: guys like that sort of thing. It's just how we're wired.

Anyway, Karen finally broke up with me and she did it in such a way that I couldn't really do anything about it. She called me and left a message, crying, saying how she couldn't go on like this anymore and that it was all her fault and that she was a mess and that she was sorry and that it was just best to quit before anyone got hurt. She was so good at her little message that I just couldn't say anything other than, "Yeah, I guess you're right, we should just quit while we're ahead." Maybe I should have fought more to keep her, but that's all just water under the bridge now. It's been about five or six years since we broke up, and she's moved out of town and she's gone, man.

But I'll always remember her and how great she was, even though she tried to cheat in the wishbone game. I bet she knew all along that you were supposed to hold the wishbone from the end and she was just messin' with me. I guess I'll never really know what happened on that fateful day, but I'll always remember two things: her cute little face and that A+ little ass she had!

Who cares if she cheated in the wishbone game? I should've just given in and let her have her way. I was such a numb skull. Man, was she hot!

Class 5 Rapids

One summer, I was back east visiting my family. We had a cabin in Millinocket, Maine, right on the lake. It was pretty nice. My stepfather was from Millinocket and every now and then he would take a little vacation up there and whoever in the family was around could come and go as they pleased.

That year, I was around, and my two stepbrothers, Alex and Matthew, attended, along with my sister Breena, and, of course, Mom was there, too.

Like usual, we were all going to go climb Mount Katahdin, which was a pretty big mountain, and not at all just a walk in the park for me. I'm not a great mountain climber, or really all that into it, but I figured I'd go along for no good reason.

My whole philosophy about my personal health has always been this: as long as I looked good, it didn't matter how healthy I was. Basically, I worked out enough to look good and I didn't care how good my cardio was, or if I could stretch much, or all the other things actual health required.

This philosophy had a few holes in it, like when it came time to go hiking on mountains with my stepbrothers who were in much better physical condition than me, even though I may have looked better.

So, we all headed off for Mount Katahdin, which, I might add, is a pretty serious mountain to climb. It's a big-ass mountain, 5,200 feet to be exact, and it's also where the Appalachian Trail begins going all the way down to Springer Mountain in Georgia.

There's a part to it called the Knife's Edge, which is about a half-a-mile long in between two peaks. It's called the Knife's Edge because from about ten miles away it looks like a jagged, nasty knife. Up close it looks like an impassible obstacle course with 30-foot boulders and crazy rocks all over the place and a 3,000-foot drop on both sides with no easy way across it.

You had to be a real mountain climber to get through the Knife's Edge. Not to mention that I'm scared of heights, and I mean SCARED of heights.

There wasn't a little trail to casually walk along with a little rope protecting people from plummeting to their deaths. There was nothin'. Just a bunch of nasty, big boulders, and you had to improvise every step carefully in order to figure out a way OVER them, or basically fall to your death. That was it.

My two stepbrothers were like mountain goats, hopping from one boulder to the next, laughing and having fun. I was in a petrified, frozen trance of uncomfortable feelings, ranging from sheer terror to remorse to hatred towards them for tricking me, once again, to come "hiking" with them.

This wasn't hiking. This was ROCK CLIMBING, with no ropes or equipment, and there was no easy way down once you were up. I was stuck up there in that God Forbidden Hell Hole called the Knife's Edge.

My one stepbrother, Matthew, whom I feel the closest to, sort of could tell I was not doing too well. He was a yoga and meditation teacher, so he was semi-aware of his surroundings, which included me clutching to a boulder, white in the face and panting in sheer terror.

I was feeling my pulse to see how high it was. It was at 180.

You know that little chart on the treadmill at the gym that shows the different age groups and the beats-per-minute pulse you should have for a good cardio work out? Well, for my age bracket, the range is around 110 to 150.

You must understand that I'm clinging to a rock, a few thousand feet up, with no safety equipment, truly scared to death of falling, for real, and to make matters worse, my heart is beating 30 beats per minute faster than the maximum allowed at the gym for a vigorous cardio workout.

I wasn't having a cardio workout. I was scared out of my mind and panicking.

My stepbrother Matt, the mindful one, somehow noticed that I wasn't doing too well and came over to me and asked if I was okay.

I looked at him and said, "Do I *look* okay to you, man? I'm dying here and I'm going to fall to my death and there's no way out. Put that in your meditation pipe and smoke it."

He tried to console me and said that he'd slow down the pace so that I might survive. The operative word was MIGHT.

While this little moment was happening, Alex sprang over, jumping like a mountain goat, not winded at all, and he was laughing. He saw me suffering, and instead of trying to help, he started throwing little rocks at me.

He just crossed the line with me, man. I was going to get him. I didn't know how, or where, or when, but I was going to get him.

You GUNKY, I thought.

In fact, the will to get Alex back gave me the strength to forge ahead. I mean, if I were to give up now and fall to my death, then there would be no sweet reward for me of getting him back somehow.

So, I found the inner strength to keep moving and I found that warrior energy spirit guide inside me, giving me the power to face my fear of dying and my fear of heights.

Those are fancy words for saying what probably really happened, which was my adrenalin from panicking kicked in, and only my will to survive, my natural instincts, allowed me to live.

Either way, I got the hell over the Knife's Edge and made it to safety. All I could think of was how and when and where I was going to get Alex back for throwing rocks at me when I was freaking out and clinging to a 3,000-foot ledge.

When we got back to the cabin, we all told our versions of our little mountain climbing expedition — kind of like when early man must've told stories about the hunt when they came back to their respective caves.

Each of us described how it went down, and when it came to me I pretty much told it like it was — that I almost died and that it was a horrible experience.

In my family, people tended to exaggerate in order to add EFFECT to their story, because quite often you'd get ignored or swept under the rug unless you could come up with a pretty convincing argument.

No one felt sorry for me because the age range of people that could cross the Knife's Edge was 11 and up. An untrained 6th grader could easily hike across the Knife's Edge, but I almost died of fear.

One time, when I was six, I was on my bicycle, trying to keep up with the big kids and they all went over a big, steep, scary hill in the back of the high school where there was sand and loose gravel at the bottom.

Of course, when I went down that thing I hit the sand and gravel and went flying and completely tore up my body in every way imaginable. I had bloody knees, elbows, hands, forehead, and other parts of my body bleeding, too. People to this day still can't figure out how I had managed to bloody so much of myself. I somehow dragged my broken body back home and my stepfather yelled at me to quit crying and take it like a man.

I was six and REALLY hurt bad.

It was his job to clean me up and fix my wounds. So, he took a really rough cloth that felt like SANDPAPER and he scrubbed my already ridiculously sensitive and hurting wounds and made them bleed more while I writhed in pain. Then, he poured on that red stuff called Mercurochrome that just made the pain worse. I almost passed out from an overload of pain and trauma.

In my house, a traumatic accident like this didn't qualify for sympathy, empathy, or even nice treatment — not even for a second. In my house, if there wasn't blood showing, then you weren't allowed to be in pain. Even if there was

233

blood showing, and in my case a LOT of blood was all over the place, I still got treated with no respect, like Rodney Dangerfield on his worst day ever.

Life isn't fair, my step-dad would say.

Whatever man, we'll talk about him later...

Back to my fun summer vacation.

It was raining that night in Millinocket, Maine and we'd heard from the locals that it had been raining for two weeks and that the rivers and lakes were really high.

We were all planning on going whitewater rafting the next day, for the first time ever, I might add. My stepbrother, Alex, was expressing some concern that maybe we should wait a few days until the water went down a little before we attempted to battle a whitewater rafting situation with untrained, first timers, like me and Matthew.

"C'mon, man," I yelled, "don't be a pussy, it'll be easy!"

He just shook his head in true fear for his life, because I guess he had some issues with raging waters, whereas I didn't care at all.

I was afraid of heights, not widths.

And, I was hoping God was going to help me, after all, and get Alex back for throwing rocks at me while I was panicking to death. This thought made a lot of sense to me and I felt really good, wallowing in my joy, knowing that he might be scared of something and bumming out about it.

For some reason, and I don't why, it seems we humans get pleasure out of other people's pain. I guess that's why there will always be wars and stuff, because someone is having a lot of fun from others' misfortunes and what not.

When we got to the river the next morning, we noticed that the water looked REALLY high. Alex didn't look too good.

I said, "It looks fine, it's only water."

So, we got to the river rafting place and we signed up for a day of rafting. We got our helmets and our little life preservers on and were just about all set.

Then, we all jumped in a big van and headed on up to

the top of the river where everyone starts. No big deal, just another day goin' raftin'.

When we arrived at the area where all the rafts were, we find out that the damn upstream was hit by lightning the night before, so it wasn't operable, which meant the water, which was already high, was out of control and what was once a Class 3 rapid was now a Class 5 rapid. Plus, all the rain from the past two weeks meant that the water was about as high as naturally possible and we were sure to get our money's worth on this river rafting expedition.

We all jumped in the little raft and met our guide. She gave us about a five-minute tutorial on how to paddle and how to lean and all the commands like, stroke faster or backstroke to turn — you know, rafting stuff.

After about five minutes of practicing, it was time to go for it. I was all excited and raring to go. Alex was looking really worried and acting all paranoid, like something bad might happen.

I was like, what could happen?

Our rafting guide asked all of us if we had ever been rafting before. We all said no. There were eight of us, plus the rafting guide in the back.

Me and Matt were in the front; we were the steering guys and point men. Alex was next to Matt and then some couple from New York and a few other randoms and that's who was in our little boat. The rafting guide looked a little nervous and said that the water was a little faster than normal and that we all needed to cooperate and do everything she said. I wasn't scared at all. I was wearing a helmet and a life preserver. It was just a little bit of water. How dangerous could it be?

Off we went!!!!

Hmmmmm.......I thought to myself, maybe this will be a teeny weeny bit scary, but probably not that big of a deal.

We were all paddling and heading into the fast part.

Stroke, stroke stroke, she yelled at us, and then she started telling us all these complicated instructions about forward, then backward and to lean and to go faster and lean.

I had no idea what she was saying.

No one could really hear her with the roar of the water. We went over an 11-foot drop...wheeeee....that was fun! That wasn't scary at all. Alex's face was all serious and he looked like he was gonna puke. I was having a blast. Me and Matt were laughing and were all exhilarated.

Then, we *really* started flying down the river and we were paddling and going sideways and the guide was yelling at us to paddle harder and for me to go backward and for my whole side to start leaning and all this stuff. We were flying along and right up ahead was a giant 15-foot drop and jagged rocks all over the place that could easily puncture the boat and kill us all.

Hey, wait a sec.

This was TOTALLY dangerous.

The guide was saying that no matter what — do NOT get out of the boat, and that if somehow we flipped, to hang on to the boat.

I was not gonna let go of this stupid boat, no matter what. I didn't want to be stuck in the middle of Class 5 rapids, getting smashed into jagged rocks everywhere.

So, we went right over the 15-foot drop, but the problem was, no one was paddling the right way and our guide was screaming at us to go forwards, and then to go backwards, and to lean and to steer and to LOOK OUT FOR THAT ROCK!!!!!!!!!!!!!!!

We went sideways over a giant water fall and smashed into a huge, jagged, mean, scary, rock.

We all screamed, "Ahhhhhhhhhhhh!!!!!!!!!!!!"

We landed, and got stuck in a backward whirlpool, which sucked the entire boat underwater.

I couldn't even see the boat; all I saw was whitewater foam pouring on our heads. The boat was completely submerged, and stuck sideways in a whirlpool at the bottom of a huge underwater cliff with millions of cold, angry gallons of water pouring on us.

I figured we would just be stuck for a few seconds and then be on our merry, wet, way. My brother Alex's face was completely white and he looked like a ghost, and he was so scared that he couldn't move. I was laughing and pointing, goofing around with my brother Matt. What was the big deal? We were just pinned on a huge rock in the middle of a whirlpool, being sucked under by the massive force of a Class 5 rapid pouring on us like thunder.

The little rafting guide girl who probably was in a lot of trouble was screaming at us to push off the rock and to paddle backward and all this other stuff we couldn't understand. We weren't going anywhere. We were totally pinned. The boat wasn't even visible and we were sideways in the middle of a Class 5 rapid, stuck and bent around a giant, mean, jagged rock. We were stuck, man, and not goin' anyplace soon.

After about five minutes, we all realized that we were REALLY stuck. This wasn't going to just go away. There were millions of pounds of force on each side of us, bending our little boat around a giant rock that was EXACTLY in the middle of the side of our boat. This situation probably was one in a million, and if we had just hit the rock slightly to the side, even an INCH, then we wouldn't be stuck. But we must've hit precisely the exact molecule right in the middle of the boat for us to be pinned like that. Oh, well, I guess we were just stuck, man.

I yelled over to Alex, who was only about four feet away, but the noise was so loud that the only way to communicate was to scream.

I said to him, "Hey, Al, you see that rock right over there? It's got your name on it, man; that's where your face is gonna be as soon as we get off this stupid boulder."

He just looked at me like a deer caught in headlights, like a mouse in a cat's mouth after it's given up squirming. He had lost his will to live and he was petrified to the point of not even being able to move or yell or do anything. He couldn't run away, he couldn't do shit, man. He was stuck with me, and I was laughing and singing and saying stuff like, "Look, no hands!" and I waved my hands in the air to show off that I was not falling out of the boat and that I was not scared and that I was having the time of my life.

About ten more minutes went by and we were super stuck, man; we were not getting out of this one on our own at all. Up on the bank on the side of the river, a team of about 10 guys showed up and threw us a big giant rope. We grabbed it and they tried to pull us out of the little whirlpool that was keeping us stuck in this waterfall situation. They couldn't pull us out; there was just too much water pouring on us, sucking us under a huge waterfall of thunderous, pounding water, gushing on our heads at all times.

About another ten minutes goes by and another team of guys showed up on the other side of the river. They threw us a rope and now we had two teams of guys trying to pull different parts of the boat around the giant stupid rock that we were pinned on.

Nothing.

We weren't going anywhere, man. After about five minutes of this, we finally got nudged off the giant rock and immediately started sprinting down the super-fast rapids.

I'm not joking when I say this was a super-fast river and there were nasty, mean, jagged rocks in all directions waiting for us to crash into them and die, right there on the spot. This was no family white water rapids for amateurs; this was a death trap, and only very experienced, professional white water rapids guys should have been *allowed* to be on that hellhole of a God forbidden river!

While the guys had been trying to pull us out, all kinds of other people gathered by the riverbank, pointing and laughing and taking pictures and using their video cameras. I guess it was pretty fun for all the landlubbers up there, watching us being pinned at the bottom of a huge waterfall.

Somehow, we managed to get our little boat to the side of the river and pulled up next to the bank, out of harm's way. Our little rafting guide chick asked if anyone wanted to get out and take the bus downstream and meet us at the BBQ area where we all were gonna have a fun little dinner.

My brother Alex sprang out of the boat and said he would meet us downstream. No one else jumped out of the boat. Not the couple from New York, not the teenage kids, not me, not Matt. Just Alex.

"Okay, bye," we said, and headed on out for the rest of the rapids.

I thought to myself how only 24 hours ago I was stuck on a super dangerous, scary, mountain ridge called the Knife's Edge and how my fear of heights was kicking my ass and there was no way to get down except to keep going forward. And how my mean brother Alex was throwing rocks at me while I was clinging to the edge of the cliff, afraid to move and feeling like dying.

How perfect this day was that we would get stuck in the middle of a Class 5 rapid and how Alex couldn't get away fast enough and was afraid of the water and of dying when really it wasn't all that dangerous, certainly not as dangerous as the rock-climbing that we had done the day before. I felt like there was justice in the Universe and that this was nature's way of getting him back. It was instant Karma, man.

We kept on cruising down the river and had a blast flying over giant drops and bouncing into huge rocks and not getting pinned again. It wasn't really all that dangerous and it was super fun.

After a very short while, we were all experts at paddling and going forward and backward, and we learned how to steer the boat really well so by the time we got to the bottom we had it down, man.

In fact, right in front of the people at the BBQ area downstream there was one last rapid and a special rock that had a backward undertow thing happening.

Our guide told us that if we hit the rapid a certain way that we could surf on the backward undertow area and actually go backward for a little bit and then get caught, intentionally, in a fun little game thing where we could control the boat going forward and backward and show off to the people in the BBQ area, who were all watching us.

I was waving to my brother Alex, who was sulking and slinking around, all scared and embarrassed and angry. Well, it served him right for throwing rocks at me when I was in a life-and-death situation.

Another cool thing that happened at the end of the day was when we returned our helmets and paddles and life jackets back at the boathouse. They had a big video projector, showing all the footage and highlights of the day.

It turned out they had a bunch of video camera people up on shore, taking videos of all the boats and people flying around on the river. Since our boat had such a dramatic thing goin' on, we had all kinds of video of us from several sources and we got to replay the whole thing, over and over, in front of my parents and all the other people's families — how we got stuck and the whole rescue with the ropes and the whole thing. It was glorious to keep the magic going on and on...

I love Class 5 rapids.

Esalen

My stepbrother, Matthew, inherited a lot of money from his grandparents and wanted to buy me a gift. Since he was a meditation and yoga teacher he wanted the gift to be in the genre of spiritual recovery and renewal. Because I live in California, he picked a place called Esalen, which is up north, near Big Sur and Monterey. I had never really heard much about the place and figured it would be fun. Little did I realize what I would be getting myself into. I found out that Esalen, with its very colorful history, means many things to many different people.

Matthew chose a Buddhist Leadership class for me and the retreat was for a whole weekend. It included a nice room and meals. I don't remember exactly why, but I needed to carpool with someone from L.A. to get there. I think my car was in the shop, like always. I used to own old, classic Mustang muscle cars. They were in the shop more often than on the road. I once owned a muscle car that was on the road for seven minutes and then spent six months in my driveway. I don't even want to get into that one, ever, really. Maybe the Buddhist Leadership class will help me from getting sidetracked in stories like this one.

Anyway, for some dumb reason, I needed a ride. I heard somehow that there was a ride sharing posting thing at Esalen, or maybe it was online or something, for people who wanted to carpool. I found some lady in Hollywood who was driving up who could give me a ride.

Remember: I had zero knowledge of Esalen and I didn't do any research on it because back then, the Internet was just starting and I don't think I even had any interest in it at the time. When the Internet first came out I thought it was stupid and like, why would anyone want to care about that? It looked like it was just for computer geeks and losers. I was stupid back then and afraid of computers, and only used computers for my studio and didn't even know how they worked.

I've come a long way, baby.

I don't remember the name of the carpool lady, or really who she was, but I do remember a few things. She picked me up on time and we shook hands and headed on out. She was probably ten years older than me, okay looking, and seemed pretty cool.

At first, that is.

It was about a four or five hour drive, so we had plenty of time to get to know each other. We started out not saying much, but it didn't take long to get into a bunch of stuff. She told me *all* about Esalen and how it came to be, etc. I didn't realize that it had such a rich history and that it was the cool hangout in the '60's for Jack Kerouac, Timothy Leary, Bob Dylan and all those stoner, druggy heroes from the good old days. She described it as basically a rich kid's house with a bunch of land on a cliff by the ocean with a bunch of drug and sex addicts running around naked, singing Kum-bay-ah. Overall, it sounded pretty cool.

By the time we got to Esalen, I'd heard enough from this chick and was glad to be getting out of her car. I can only take about three or four hours of hanging out in a closed environment with a wacky chick before it just gets old, man. Maybe if she was a little younger and hotter I could have been able to hang a little bit better, but she was really getting on my nerves towards the end of the trip.

She told me that she wasn't going back to L.A. after her stay at Esalen and that I had to find a ride back. She said it would be easy and that people were always getting rides back to L.A. and that I would have no trouble.

I found my way to where I was supposed to check in and got my room key. I was supposed to have a roommate, but he wasn't there yet.

I had a little time to kill and started poking around a

little, like I always do when I'm somewhere new. The actual place that I was staying at was really nice; it looked like a big old house with about 20 rooms and a big downstairs living room where the class was going to be. It sort of looked like a big old bed and breakfast joint.

Since I was a little bit early, the guys running the weekend class were downstairs in the big living room, frantically organizing all their little papers and posters and graphs and stuff. I walked in and said hi and asked them if they were the leadership guys and they said they were. They looked a little annoyed and nervous because they weren't quite ready and I was early and all eager and happy. Then I asked them if I could help. They said I could, and gave me a pile of papers to sort and put in folders. They had 100's of pages with all kinds of little exercises and questions and diagrams.

I sat on the floor by the big fireplace and started organizing the leadership class workshop papers. After about ten minutes, a few more people from the leadership class wandered in and I said they should come on over and help me organize the big mess of papers on the floor.

The two leadership class teachers were trying to lay low and not say anything because they didn't want to look like they were disorganized or behind schedule. So, I just sort of started telling everyone what to do and they all jumped in with me and we had a blast sitting on the floor putting all the little pages together in their little folders.

Maybe the two leadership class teachers were secretly testing us to see who the leaders were in the class by pretending that they weren't very good leaders. Because, aren't good leaders supposed to be organized and have all their homework done BEFORE they go to Esalen and teach a leadership class?

I recently went on the Internet and looked up Esalen and did a little research about the place. Apparently, just about anyone can teach little workshops and classes there on just about anything, from jumping around and singing, to yoga and meditation.

243

I found out that each teacher gets to stay there for free and also gets $75 per person who signs up for the class. I guess as long as you can get at least eight people to sign up for the class, no matter what it is, you get to stay there for free and get paid.

Maybe the two leadership class teachers just wanted to make a few bucks and hang out there at the aging hippie spa and get free meals. Esalen is kind of like a spiritual, trippy resort for rich, aging hippies who listen to the Grateful Dead, who eat politically correct rice, and pretend that they're down with the people.

Anyway, back to the story....

As usual, I gravitated towards the pretty girls in the group and made friends right away with them. It didn't take long, either. Just because it was a leadership class didn't mean that we weren't supposed to have fun and potentially have hookups with chicks, man. There were about 20 of us altogether and it was just a nice bunch of people. I don't really remember learning anything about leadership, or Zen, or anything of importance, but I do remember that it was fun and the whole Esalen experience was nice overall.

Some of the Buddhist Leadership workshop was about sitting in a big circle with the two leadership guys in the middle. They would ask all of us random questions and we would go around the circle, one by one, and say stuff.

In a way, it was really nothing more than organized hanging out.

In another section of the workshop, the leadership guys would single out someone and do a little "one-on-one" in front of the whole group. There were little sayings, and little "wins" and little "breakthroughs" about this and that, but I really thought it was mostly entertainment and just for fun.

After a long, hard day of organized hanging out and pointing at diagrams on the wall about leadership, it was time for dinner. We all headed out to find where the dinner place was. Esalen is a physically beautiful place and it's nice just to walk around and be by the ocean in that part of northern California.

We eventually found the building where everyone goes to have meals. It was sort of like a fancy summer camp-vibe, mess hall with artsy-fartsy people of all different types. You know, lots of granola people, vegetarians, and hippies, young and old.

It was a pretty cool place — to visit, that is. I wouldn't want to make it a permanent lifestyle choice. That would be extremely strange on a full-time basis.

Of course, whenever I'm in a new place I start to snoop around and take notice of all the little details and check things out and make little observations. I noticed that there was a lot of politically correct food all over the place. I think there was something like eight different kinds of health food rice and many varieties of tofu and beans and salads and all sorts of healthy stuff.

It was clear that the food was making a real statement about Esalen, and that it was trying REAL hard to say that they were healthy people and mindful, conscious eaters, and food preparers. There were all kinds of vegan stuff and vegetarian stuff and just a bunch of different things to eat for all the different types of health food people there.

I wasn't really a health food nut, but I thought it was mildly entertaining to see how hard everyone was trying to be healthy. In all fairness, the food was pretty darn good and quite mindfully prepared.

Some people say that when you prepare food, the actual thoughts you have affect the taste. Then again, maybe the actual thoughts we have doing ANYTHING might have an effect on the outcome of the thing we're doing, above and beyond the actual thing we're doing.

Like, if you're fishing and think scary, mean fish thoughts maybe the fish won't cooperate as much and let you kill them for fun or eat them. Or, perhaps I'm over thinking the actual process of thinking and maybe it doesn't really make as much difference as I think. Or, maybe it does for some things, and not for others, and probably there's a happy medium in the middle, like most things.

I did notice that way off in the back of the big dining room there was a little teeny-weeny sign that said "Coffee and Cigarettes" so I immediately had to check out that area, just to see how the health food people would present that part of the show.

They had a very bustling, thriving little robust business going on with the organic coffee and trendy little fancy cappuccino drinks (all very mindfully prepared with only the finest, 100% certified organic and range-free coffee beans, etc.). You could get beer and wine and hard alcohol drinks if you wanted, as well.

Then, I noticed they had all kinds of little candy bars that said "Save the Rhino's" on the back of the wrapper, and that a certain percent of the proceeds would go to saving specific endangered species, etc.

I wonder how many rhinos got saved by the candy eating health food people? I guess I'll never know for sure if any rhinos ever got saved, or if it could be proven that the money really went to saving any of them. Maybe I'm just being skeptical or jaded or something, but maybe, just maybe, the Esalen people are trying a little too hard to be politically correct about too many things. But hey, maybe the rhinos needed to be saved by the Esalen candy eaters, and I might just be wrong about the whole thing.

I met all kinds of cool people and had a lot of amazing conversations with all sorts of types. There was no shortage of interesting characters floating around that joint.

After dinner, all the little cliques formed and it didn't take long for certain people to gravitate towards certain others. It's funny how in social situations it really just comes down to basic, human behaviors, like the pretty girls wanting to be around the big guys, or the rich guys, or whatever.

Nothing has probably changed since caveman times, other than little details, like hairstyles and stuff. People are pretty much people wherever you go and it doesn't matter what color, or race, or size, or where in the world you're from. We all just want to have a good time and be well liked and not get into too much trouble while we're at it.

Of course there are exceptions to every rule, but, in general, this is what I have noticed in my life.

After dinner, and whatever politically correct desserts they were serving, everyone all seemed to know what the next thing was to do. I had NO idea, so I just sort of tagged along.

Everyone except me knew about going to the outdoor hot springs down by the edge of the cliff near the ocean. That sounded like fun. How cool was that, to have outdoor natural hot springs bubbling up from the ground, outside, right by the edge of a big cliff near the ocean?

I just cruised along with everyone else from my leadership workshop and headed off for the hot springs. I did notice, however, that it seemed like everyone was pretty psyched to go and that they all looked like they knew how much fun it was going to be, and I just sort of sensed that it was an extra special fun place.

We all trotted off down a dimly lit, outdoor path, leading to the edge of the cliff where there were some cool, little, old buildings where it looked like you could get massages and stuff. I was with two or three of the prettiest women there and we were all getting along really nicely and talking about spirituality and past lives and karma and neat things like that. I just felt really lucky and happy to be hanging out with such interesting, pretty women who were on a spiritual quest like I was and that everything just seemed so special and neat all over the place.

We all headed in to the main building where there were lockers and bathrooms and stuff, and I just kinda went in and, like usual, I pretended I knew where everything was. We grabbed some towels and everyone just started taking off their clothes and headed off for the showers. There was only one room with showers and the locker room area was for both men and women.

It took me about three seconds to figure out what was going on. I instantly pulled my clothes off like I'd been there a million times before and I hopped into the shower room right next to the two prettiest girls. All of us in my workshop class were there —NAKED — acting like it was the most normal and natural thing.

No one said anything funny about it, and naturally, I pretended that I knew all about it and just went about my business and took a nice hot shower. Of course, I was standing next to the two prettiest, NAKED women from my class whom I had just met that day, and my teachers were there standing next to their favorite, NAKED women and it all just sort of seemed to unfold, naturally, without anyone saying anything about the fact that we were all NAKED and complete strangers in the middle of a shower room! NAKED!

After we all took our quick little showers, we headed off to the hot springs. I saw a little sign by the door to the outside area where the hot springs were that said in small letters, "Clothing Optional."

I guess if you wore a bathing suit at a nudist colony in an outdoor hot spring you might kinda look like a nerd or a square. I thought it was mildly amusing that they had a sign saying it was optional to wear clothes or not, like anyone ever, in the history of Esalen, wore a bathing suit there. It turns out that Esalen is internationally known for its naked hot springs area and that's the sort of not-talked-about thing that everyone seems to know about, except me — at the time, that is.

I caught on pretty quick though, and I didn't even flinch. I suppose I'm not all that unique, in a way. I guess just about any red-blooded guy who was hanging out with a bunch of pretty girls at a weekend workshop in a beautiful, luxurious place by the ocean would probably have reacted the same way once he realized all the girls were getting naked, right in front of everyone.

Maybe it should be like that everywhere, or maybe not. I guess if it were like that everywhere, then it wouldn't be as special when it did happen. I suppose, in life, we need to have these contrasts; otherwise we wouldn't want to risk having the world be a Utopia because that would be too boring for the war people.

There are the "make-love-not-war" people and there are the "think tank" guys from Halliburton and Raytheon who love making 11 trillion dollars for random acts of violence against people who didn't do anything.

I guess the only way to stop wars would be to find out ways to make a bigger profit from peace. It's probably been that way since caveman times and just the weapons, hairstyles, and fake reasons for war have changed.

The hot springs were amazing. There were about five of them all lined up by the edge of a big cliff above the ocean. Steam was rising from them and all kinds of funny mineral smells were oozing up as well. Once you got used to it, which didn't take long, it all just kind of worked.

And, being naked with a bunch of strangers in a natural hot spring, under the stars in the dark moonlight by the sea, is pretty darn fun. There wasn't any hanky-panky going on at all; it was just a nice, fun way to hang out and relax.

I ended up sitting next to a woman who was about ten years older than I was, and she was really cool. She said that she was Ted Turner's right-hand woman and a big-time executive for that TV network. She and I got along really well and as we talked and learned about one another, one thing led to another until a rather funny thing happened. I told her that I was a musician and she said she knew a lot of musicians in L.A. and then I told her that I had gone to Berklee in Boston and then she started mentioning names and I did, too, and then we found out that we both knew someone in common.

I knew this kid back at school named Dan and he was a bass player and she knew him as well, because she was his Dad's girlfriend for years! I was sitting naked, in a hot spring next to my friend's step mom! It was a small-world moment and she was really cool; so whatever, we were just friends anyways and nothing more happened.

The next morning I called my brother, Matthew, (the one who paid for the workshop) and told him I was having a blast. He said that he knew some people who were working there for a few months in exchange for being able to live there and do workshops and yoga and hang out in the naked hot springs. I guess, in a way, that's not a bad way to live. He told me who they were and what they looked like and how to find them and to say hello from Matthew. So, I thanked him again and then headed off for breakfast.

I had now been in that place for a good 12 hours and pretty much knew where everything was; where all the bathrooms were, where the dining room was, where the massage area was, where the hot springs were etc.

I was an old pro and feeling all confident and secure about my surroundings.

I walked into the dining room all by myself to get in line for breakfast. The food was amazing, as always, and there was an abundance of things to try. Everything was all healthy and good for you and I was really getting into the vibe of the place.

Of course, for fun, I always like to analyze places and

try to find things wrong or what I consider to be funny, which isn't necessarily what others might think of as funny. This place was no exception. I noticed that there were a lot of similar types of people trying really hard to be individuals. A lot of the younger people had longer hair, and played hacky sack and looked like they were all Grateful Dead heads. They all had really expensive, designer hiking boots, and the same brand of knapsacks, and I just kept noticing more and more how exactly the same they all looked and acted, even though the premise was that they were supposed to be individual people.

Same thing with the older people; they all had their little Grateful Dead t-shirts, and tie-dyed outfits and expensive shoes and what not — probably the parents of those rich, hippie kids.

I bet the guys who drive old Volkswagen vans with the peace signs really drive new BMW's and Cadillac's back home. They just keep their old vans around as props so when they go to Esalen they look like they're still part of the '60's and keeping the dream alive.

I was a small boy during the '60's and missed out on seeing the Beatles, Hendrix, The Doors and Janis Joplin. However, three out of those four bands have musicians, who have all died from drug or alcohol related over doses. It seems to me that dying from self indulgent abuse of drugs and alcohol isn't very hip, cool or about peace and love.

The music those people made was wonderful, but I try to separate the difference between blanket statements that the '60's were all about peace and love when the fact is, a lot of people tragically committed suicide because they were lonely and confused.

I remember reading an article in *Rolling Stone* magazine where Mick Jagger was asked if he could sum up the '60's in one sentence. He said the entire peace and love movement was about wide ties and bellbottoms.

I think Esalen got it right. Peace and love works best when everyone's NAKED.

The Stand-Up Comic

I was thumbing through a course book for L.A. City College one night and came across something that looked like fun –– stand-up comedy.

It was only four classes and it only cost $70. I could afford that. Plus, it was only once a week for two hours at night. That was not a big commitment time-wise, so I figured I might try it. I had always liked the idea of trying to do stand-up.

I have always liked a good challenge.

I thought I'd start my stand up like this:

"Ladies and gentlemen, I want to thank you for coming to my stand up comedy presentation. I was thinking it would be fun to do something scary, because I'm always on the lookout for something challenging and it was a toss-up between taking a stand up comedy class or skydiving. I thought to myself, *What if I chose the sky diving class, and as I jumped out of the plane, I realized I'd forgotten my parachute? I would hate that feeling of knowing during a good ten minutes of falling and bumming that I should have just taken that stupid comedy claaaaasaaaaassssssss, as I fell to my death.*"

That probably would've been a funny way to start a stand-up comedy bit. But, since I had zero experience being a stand-up comic, I really didn't know what would work or what wouldn't.

So, I picked the stand-up comedy class instead of the sky diving class; I figured, if I screwed up in the comedy class I would at least not physically die, like I might with skydiving. That would be a terrible way to go, just falling and knowing that there was no way out of it and that it would be a few minutes of falling and then I would splat on the ground and for the first millisecond I would feel it and it would really hurt, before the lights went out permanently. What a yucky feeling that would be, all the way dooooooooooown.

Then again, I guess a worse feeling would be if I was stuck in a fire in a big building when it was burning and I was trying to decide if I should die burning to death in a horrible, slow agonizing way, or jump out the window.
Fortunately, I haven't had to choose a fate like that.

Actually, I just found out from a friend the other day that, according to him, some secret survey was taken and the number one thing most people were afraid of was public speaking. Fear of actual death, was only number seven. So, people would rather DIE, than speak in public, which is the same thing as stand-up comedy, sort of. So, in a way, I tried to do something that was scarier than actual death, at least for some people.

I signed up for the stand-up comedy class and paid my little $70 and marked it in my calendar.
The night finally came, and I drove on over to the L.A. City College campus and found out where to go and showed up. It was a pretty dirty and beat-up campus, nothing like the one I grew up around at Dartmouth, an Ivy League campus full of rich kids, which was absolutely beautiful everywhere.
This was just an inner city college campus of beat-up old buildings, dingy old shrubbery, and crappy stuff everywhere. But it was a beginning, a start, and who was I to judge that place anyways? I figured it would be the least intimidating place on the planet. I figured it would be just a bunch of random people in a little classroom and that I would be the best, by far, and that I could easily handle something like that. I really didn't know what to expect, other than it was only $70, and if it stunk, I would just write it off as another bad experiment in life that didn't work out, like all the other times.
I found the room and walked in and sat in the back. There were about 20 students in the classroom once everyone filed in. The age range was about 25 to 60, all sizes and shapes, men and women, housewives, random people, black, white,

Mexican, pretty much a little cross section of America right there, sittin' around me.

My fellow students didn't look all that smart or funny and I was not at all scared to be in the classroom with them. The teacher was all angry and bitter about having to teach a comedy class to loser, wanna-be comedians.

It wasn't a very intimidating class, that's for sure. A lot of the students would just rant and rave about their bad childhoods. I guess comedy for some people is just a cheap form of therapy, or maybe they have a thing for abuse, or maybe a little of both.

Then again, comedians may just be crazy people who get a break and find an angle for making things funny. Who knows? This was just a simple four session, stupid comedy class, and for our final "paper" we had to do a gig at the *Ice House* in Pasadena.

The problem was, I have an intense fear of public speaking and can't even make a toast at a wedding or anything like that. So, to go up on stage, in front of strangers for ten minutes, by myself, and try to make them laugh is probably a pretty big jump for an agoraphobic, introverted extrovert like me.

But I did it anyways.

Probably because when I was a kid, I told myself that I wanted to be whatever was the hardest thing I could find. I guess having a stepfather who was the debate team captain at Harvard, a professional speaker and on the lecture circuit, and basically a narcissistic personality type might've exacerbated my little fear of public speaking.

One can only speculate.

I figured that a stand-up comedy class would be the perfect thing to overcome my fear of public speaking; I mean, how hard could it be?

One of the guys in the class was Christian Slater's father. He introduced himself as Christian Slater's father and went on a ten-minute rant about how his son wouldn't help him get any work and that he was a no-good kid and how fucked up his life was, etc. It was actually pretty entertaining listening to this poor old guy.

There were school teachers there and fat housewives, and skinny Asian girls who talked about being immigrants in Hollywood with 24 of their relatives in a one-bedroom apartment and how the toilet couldn't handle all that pooh, and so there was pooh all over the tub and it was GROSS, man!

The class was a lot of regular people all wanting to be stand-up comics because somewhere someone must have said they were funny.

I know I'm funny, because I can make people laugh all the time. I do it even when I'm NOT trying to make them laugh. They laugh even harder during those times because the subject matter of what I say is funny, and of course my delivery is impeccable.

The subject of my funny stuff is simply this: true stories of how things have gone wrong in my life. That's it. Since SO many things have gone wrong in my life, I literally have four hours of nonstop material.

I've been conned, ripped off, lied to, cheated, fired, blamed for things I didn't do, busted, grounded, lost, blackmailed, threatened to be killed, attacked, chased, molested, abandoned, sold out, scared to death, framed; you name it, I've been at the butt-end of it.

Since I'm such a super evolved and positive person, I've learned how to make the best of it and use it as material for my stand-up act.

My favorite self-help book slogan for this type of situation is, "Turning Stumbling Blocks into Stepping Stones."

I have no shortage of messed-up things that have happened to me, which I can remember in Technicolor detail for some weird reason, and I don't mind sharing them with you, the friendly reader.

When I visit with my therapist, I usually practice my stand-up material with him, because so many bad things happen to me and the way I tell the stories always cracks up my therapist.

It's actually really fun going to my therapist; all I do is try out new jokes on him and tell true stories. Fortunately for me, most of my stories sound so far-fetched that people assume they're made up. Little do they realize that they're actually 99% true.

There was this one guy in class that was a total psycho and cracked me up. He was bald, probably in his mid 40's, and was always sweating and really hyper. He'd get up in front of the class and do his act and he was so bizarre and strange. He would tell a really stupid joke, and make a really dumb face, and then sprint to the other side of the room and tell another stupid joke, make another crazy face, and sprint back to where he started. Over and over, he'd be running and sprinting and sweating and joking and grimacing. He was way out there.

There was also this really funny, depressed, angry Englishman, with the great accent and the whole bit. He would tell his English jokes and was super funny, but he would always be putting himself down after his jokes (not to be funny, but for real), and then apologize for not being funny (which the whole time was really funny), and then say how he shouldn't be trying this and who was he kidding, etc.

I would talk with him after class and say, "Man, you gotta incorporate your low self-esteem into your act. It's really funny. No one will know that you aren't really pretending to be all bummed out and self-loathing. You might as well cash in on his negativity because if you're gonna be that way anyways, why not make a buck out of it?"

He ended up flaking on the final test –– our live show at the Ice House in Pasadena. I was hoping that he would've had the balls to show up, but he didn't. Let me tell you, oh fine reader, it takes BALLS to do stand up when you're afraid of speaking in public, or when you're afraid, in general, to speak up at all, and then to do it all publicly at a comedy club in front of a REAL audience.

I'm serious, man; it's no JOKE, being a stand-up comic. It's scary as hell. Because let's just be honest: most of these people in my stupid L.A. Community College four hour comedy class were just a bunch of would-be-loser-comic-schmucks.

But the class was fun, and I was probably in the "more funny" category with about five others. We all knew who we were and we all stuck together. The funny people know who they are in life, in general, and maybe they stick together or maybe they don't, but in this class, we stuck together.

I had a video camera that I used to practice with. It was a really good tool. I'd do stand up in my living room with a microphone and just start going and going. I would do about 45 minutes of stand up and then stop and watch the magic unfold. I thought the WHOLE thing was funny, which made it hard to tell what other people would like, because, quite frankly, it really didn't matter what I thought, because I was not the audience. YOU are. If I think everything I say is funny and no one else does, then that just makes me crazy, and everyone knows that crazy people don't make very much money. Well, some of them do, but they're crazy in different ways than stand-up comedy, or maybe they're good at something that pays a lot, and then they act crazy later, or something.

Either way, I knew that in order for me to pull off this comedy thing, I would have to pick my best material. Plus, I only had ten minutes on stage, so I had to pick SOMETHING. I kind of had an idea of what was my best material and sort of created my act.

I called my ex-girlfriend Karen, a professional stage actress who could do everything, including comedy. I figured she would be a good person to show some of my ideas. She said it was cool, to come over and bring my video camera and do my thing.

So, I went over there and stood in front of her and my little video camera and proceeded to tell her a bunch of funny stories. She cracked up all the way through most of it and after about 45 minutes, I stopped.

She told me what she liked the best and what she thought worked the best and told me what to cut out and all that good stuff. It really helped.

I, of course, was careful NOT to bring up the wishbone incident in my act in front of her, because she was in that story and I figured that it wouldn't be wise to make fun of her right to her face.

Which makes me wonder –– what if I joke on people and they show up at my gigs? Then what? What if I joke on my family members and someone shows up? I guess I'll just have to cross that bridge when I get there.

The time came to do our big show at the world famous *Ice House* in Pasadena, California. Only about half of the class showed up. The rest just chickened out.

I was pretty confident that I would do okay. I figured if I didn't faint, actually pass out, and if I got just ONE laugh, I would be a success. That's all I really wanted, was to not faint, and get ONE laugh.

I had invited a few friends and my old pal Brentley and his girlfriend were there. At least someone showed up to see me, and that's all that mattered. There were about 50 other people in the audience plus our class and their friends and family so it was a pretty decent turnout. I brought my video camera to document this momentous event, and I'm glad I did.

When it was my turn, I was so scared and nervous. I was just hating life.

I went up there and the dumb M.C. pronounced my name wrong. Not off to a good start.

My first couple of dumb stories didn't get any laughs at all. I was bombing. I knew it, the audience knew it, and we were stuck with each other for the next ten minutes.

Eventually, I warmed up and got a couple little teeny-weeny laughs here and there, and then I started doing well and got a bunch of good, solid laughs and I felt like I could handle any situation in life.

Man, if I can do stand-up, I can do ANYTHING!

I did my little ten-minute act. I didn't get booed off the stage and no one threw rotten tomatoes at me and no one heckled me or yelled at me. I went up there and I did what I was supposed to do and I didn't suck. That was the main thing: as long as I didn't suck, I was a success.

I suppose preparing for all those hours and spending all that time memorizing all that stuff probably had an influence on how good my act was. Maybe that was the key. Maybe I just needed to work hard at it and then it would get better! What a concept.

A couple months later, I met this girl who was a stand-up comic at one of my 12-step meetings. She shared about being a stand-up comic and that she had her very own show every Wednesday night. I came up to her after the meeting and told her that I was a closet case stand-up comic and was wondering if she would let me audition for her show. She laughed and said that I was funny and that I passed the test already. Little did I know what kind of show I was getting myself into.

It turns out that she had a show at Lucy's Laundromat on Sunset Blvd. in Silverlake (just east of Hollywood). It's sort of a hipster part of town. My friend calls it Sliverflake, not sure why though...! Anyway, so I guess it really was in a laundromat. So, I go to Lucy's Laundromat and there is the girl from the meeting with a little microphone set up right in front of the unisex bathroom. It was actually a pretty fancy Laundromat because it had a Subway and a Starbucks built into the place. So, she must have made a deal with the Laundromat somehow to  let her do a little one hour show to entertain the Laundry people and the Subway eaters and Starbucks drinkers. It was actually pretty cool.

There were about 9 or 10 other would-be stand-up comics there and we had our little area and some chairs lined up to accommodate maybe 15 people. It was the big time man! I had arrived. I had a regular gig doing stand-up comedy every Wednesday where I could work on my *CRAFT*. Life couldn't be better. One of the guys in our group would just get up there and make funny sounds, like from a penny whistle; the little plastic wind instrument in grade school that has a slider thing on it that goes up and down in pitch. He thought that was pretty clever, to make funny sounds. I laughed, for the first ten seconds. Then it got old FAST.

There were some other comics that were pretty funny though. I have to admit that a few of them were seasoned pro's. Not me. I may be a lot of things, but a seasoned professional stand-up comic I ain't. But, it was worth a try. For a while, that is...

So, now it's my turn and I get up there, on the mic, in front of about 8 people and a few straggler Laundromat people. Watching, and waiting to be entertained, by me, Cliff Brodsky. The Professional Stand-Up Comic. That's how I wanted to be introduced. Keep in mind that perception is 9/10's of reality; if those people think I think that I'm funny, then at least I have a CHANCE of making them laugh. The problem is, that I didn't know any jokes. I knew a lot of other peoples jokes, and I could recite entire George Carlin and Bill Cosby and Monty Python records from front to back. But I had no jokes. What I did have, were funny stories. That was going to be my angle. I would pretend to tell jokes and really just tell wacky stories that SEEMED like jokes if you didn't know me, because they were such bizarre stories. Unfortunately for me, the first thing I would say once I got up there was a confession that I wasn't really a stand-up comic and that I only knew strange true stories (which no one believed me, because they thought I was a comic pretending to not know what I was doing)...which actually worked pretty well as a formula. I bet a LOT of comics do that, just pretend to be crazy (when in reality they are NOT pretending), but we, the stupid audience think they are genius's. Who know's really what comedy audiences are thinking about. Probably the same thing as other audiences: when am I going to get laid and is there any food around. It pretty much comes down to those TWO THINGS. Not much has changed in the past million years for us humans, sad to admit.

Long story short: I get up there and do my usual bits about getting yelled at as a rock 'n' roll roadie and how I gave

260

the finger to communist Germans going through check point Charlie back in '89 and how I smuggled weed into Berlin from Amsterdam and how I got fired from the tour manager...you know...funny story material. I got a bunch of laughs, not really because of my genius story telling, but probably because I am a little bit funny when I get nervous and try to remember TRUE stories that everyone in the audience thinks I WROTE.

While I was doing my stand-up act, I noticed that there was blood on the floor right in front of me and I stopped my act and pointed out that there was real blood on the floor and what the hell kind of Laundromat was this! Laugh laugh laugh...tee hee hee...they thought I was SO funny. I wasn't telling a joke, I was merely pointing out that someone must have gotten stabbed recently and that this was a pretty tough Laundromat.

I only went back one more time at Lucy's Laundromat, because I could see that I wasn't really going to get anywhere in my stand-up career. At some point, I'm just going to have to get over my fear of public speaking and go do a real open mic night somewhere in Hollywood and just go for it.

I actually have written a few jokes lately. I only have three jokes right now. One of them goes like this: "what if there was a band called The Mexican Beatles, they would be Juan, Raul, Gorge (pronounced 'whore hey'), and Gringo!"

I also have a bit that I want to do someday. What if Elvis Presley was still alive and that he went to AA meetings; what would his name be? Twelvis Stepley! I could do a rock n roll impression of Twelvis Stepley singing about drugs and alcohol and sobriety. Maybe that would be funny. Who knows.

I always said when I was a kid that I wanted to do the hardest thing I could think of. I wanted to do the most difficult and challenging thing. Nuclear Physicist...too easy. Ivy League Professor...nope. President of the United States...wouldn't take that job if you paid me a million dollars. To me, it takes real courage and I mean REAL courage to get up there and try to make people laugh, as a profession, with your own hand written jokes.

Marines, Navy Seals, Mafia, Hit Men...most people think those people have a lot of courage. Maybe they do and maybe they don't. To me, being a stand-up comedian is the scariest possible job I can think of right now.

We should all have a moment of silence for the unsung stand-up comic.

They are the REAL heroes in life.